Saddleworth

Discovery Walks

with **CHRISTIAN MAYLOR**

Maps: © Christian Maylor
Photography: © Ray Green

All of the photographs contained in this book are available for purchase at:
www.raygreenphotography.co.uk

Printed and bound by CPI Group (UK) Ltd, Croydon, CR0 4YY
A CIP catalogue record for this book is available from the British Library.

JOURNEYMAN

Published in 2014 by Journeyman Guides
113 Broadway, Royton, Oldham, Lancashire, OL2 5BW
www.saddleworthdiscoverywalks.co.uk
ISBN 978-0-9930100-0-2

Contents

Foreword

As a professional climber I've been lucky to see many of the world's most dramatic outdoor regions. Alaska, Patagonia, the Himalayan heights, Yosemite, Canada's wild lands and even Pitcairn island: all abound with beauty, yet our own region does not differ in granting charm and incentive to head out of the door.

I have always upheld that Saddleworth offers a unique balance on our planet. A small step from civilisation leads to some beautiful and rugged terrain. Striding out into such a striking back garden is a luxury few can enjoy. Whether you choose a calm autumn stroll, absorbing the abundance of colours along the canal, or a trek over the moorland summits, rewarding vistas will become ingrained. For a quick getaway, a lap around Dovestone Reservoir or a more ambitious climb up to Indian's Head (Wimberry Rocks) should serve to flush out the day-to-day worries, with woes easily left behind. For those wanting a full day's outing, there are miles upon miles of footpaths to be explored. Whether revelling in a warm summer's breeze or imprinting your footsteps in a winter's fresh snowfall, the character is never the same, even upon a familiar path. Enriched by each seasonal shift, the atmosphere always subtly changes its reward.

Incidentally, for a recent grand tour down the Pennine Way, from Scotland back home, we were granted such fine weather that a tent was never erected, and each night was spent under the stars. Seeing Saddleworth's familiar terrain at the end of much moorland time proved quite an ecstatic moment. But one needn't travel so far: simply watching the evening sun cast its blanket of golden rays across Chew Valley's west-facing flanks whilst stood atop Alphin Pike's lofty vantage point offers incentive enough for anyone treading upon the hill's crest.

I mentioned the Pennine Way due to it feeling like it completes a circle in many ways. Initial Sunday treks exploring Saddleworth's varied landscape led to seeking out the crags and their slice of steep adventure, creating a climber out of me; yet when atop the Pennines travelling south, I was reminded of those first rich feelings established from simply stepping out of the door and exploring Saddleworth's beautiful countryside, with a sparkle of discovery around every corner. Later in life, outings with Oldham Outdoor Pursuits allowed me the gift of seeing the wonder in the eyes and beaming smiles of those enjoying their first experiences beyond the urban sprawl.

Personally, I feel that I have been incredibly fortunate to have had such a wonderful environment as Saddleworth in which to take my first outdoor steps, and I wouldn't trade that for anything.

Kevin Thaw
Professional climber and mountaineer

General Information

About the walks

All of the walks detailed within this book are circular and use legal rights of way, permissive footpaths or open access land. Before undertaking any walks, always ensure that routes are free from any restrictions and that legal access is still in place.

Each walk contains a route description and an informative sketch map, along with information about points of interest which can be seen en route. Route descriptions are intended not be too restrictive and, if so desired, the reader should feel free to vary the route in order to explore and discover more of Saddleworth's dramatic landscape and rich history, just as I did when writing this book.

Time and distance

Guide times stated for each walk are generous and are calculated using an average pace of approximately 4km per hour / 2.5 miles per hour, with time allowed for overall ascent, nature of terrain and time spent exploring points of interest. Distances and ascent have been calculated from the map and should be treated as guidelines only.

Navigation

The sketch maps contained in this book are for illustration purposes only. This guidebook should be used in conjunction with the relevant Ordnance Survey Explorer series maps, as detailed for each walk. The reader should ensure that they have adequate navigational knowledge and experience to undertake the walks detailed in this book.

Anyone wishing to learn, or improve, mountain navigation skills can contact the author to arrange bespoke training. info@saddleworthdiscoverywalks.co.uk

The walks in this book are covered by:
OS Explorer (1:25,000) OL1: The Peak District – Dark Peak Area
OS Explorer (1:25,000) OL21: South Pennines
OS Explorer (1:25,000) 277: Manchester & Salford

Safety

The reader should ensure that they have suitable experience for undertaking the walks described. Many of the walks cover high, exposed and remote terrain, and suitable clothing and footwear should be worn according to the weather conditions, time of year and terrain.

Countryside Code

- Respect the life and work of the countryside
- Leave gates and property as you find them
- Protect plants and animals
- Take all of your litter home
- Guard against all risks of fire
- Keep dogs under effective control
- Consider other people and local landowners
- Keep to rights of way and open access land

Mountain Rescue

In an emergency dial 999 and ask for POLICE. Tell the controller that you require MOUNTAIN RESCUE. Give as much detailed information as possible, including an accurate six figure grid reference.

Map Symbols

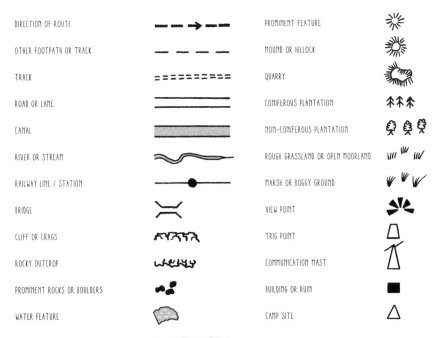

DIRECTION OF ROUTE	PROMINENT FEATURE
OTHER FOOTPATH OR TRACK	MOUND OR HILLOCK
TRACK	QUARRY
ROAD OR LANE	CONIFEROUS PLANTATION
CANAL	NON-CONIFEROUS PLANTATION
RIVER OR STREAM	ROUGH GRASSLAND OR OPEN MOORLAND
RAILWAY LINE / STATION	MARSH OR BOGGY GROUND
BRIDGE	VIEW POINT
CLIFF OR CRAGS	TRIG POINT
ROCKY OUTCROP	COMMUNICATION MAST
PROMINENT ROCKS OR BOULDERS	BUILDING OR RUIN
WATER FEATURE	CAMP SITE

STEEP GROUND, EDGE, RIDGELINE OR EMBANKMENT

Introduction

Saddleworth is a remote, picturesque upland region nestled amongst the western flanks of the Pennine Hills and lying on the northern edges of the Peak District National Park. Sitting on the former border of Yorkshire and Lancashire, the area was formerly part of the ancient West Riding of Yorkshire. Consisting of wild, windswept moors, rocky outcrops and rugged glaciated valleys, Saddleworth is a popular playground for walkers, climbers, mountain-bikers, fell-runners and other outdoor enthusiasts.

The earliest documented evidence of Saddleworth is found in the Domesday Book, in which it is referred to as 'Quick', and references to Saddleworth's former name are still evident today. However, the area's rich history dates back to the Stone Age, and there is clear evidence of human habitation since this time. Place names made up of Celtic, Norse and Anglian dialect are proof that the area has been settled by numerous foreign 'visitors'. During the early Roman occupation of Britain, Saddleworth was once the northernmost frontier of Rome's vast empire.

Long before the industrial revolution, Saddleworth was an important area for domestic wool and textile weaving, and many surviving examples of stone weavers' cottages can still be seen throughout the area. During the 'cotton boom', Saddleworth became an important centre for textile production, and an abundance of large mills were built to cash in on the world's insatiable demand for cotton.

This lost corner of the former West Riding of Yorkshire consists of several picturesque villages, all of which have their own unique individual characters and local traditions, which have instilled a strong sense of community. The area's rugged moors and beautiful valleys are criss-crossed by a vast network of footpaths, bridleways and ancient packhorse trails, which allow the walker virtual unrestricted access to enjoy the area's wonderful landscape whilst learning about its history, culture and people.

NORTH

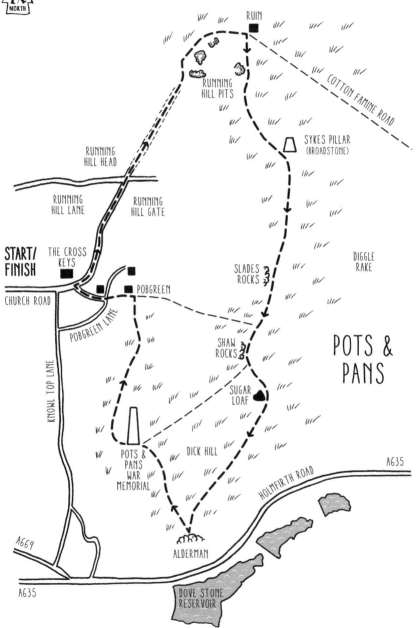

RUIN

RUNNING HILL PITS

COTTON FAMINE ROAD

SYKES PILLAR
(BROADSTONE)

RUNNING HILL HEAD

RUNNING HILL LANE

RUNNING HILL GATE

DIGGLE RAKE

START/ FINISH

THE CROSS KEYS

SLADES ROCKS

POBGREEN

CHURCH ROAD

POBGREEN LANE

SHAW ROCKS

POTS & PANS

KNOWL TOP LANE

SUGAR LOAF

POTS & PANS WAR MEMORIAL

DICK HILL

A635

HOLMFIRTH ROAD

A669

ALDERMAN

A635

DOVE STONE RESERVOIR

Pots & Pans

Start/Finish: *Cross Keys Inn, Running Hill Gate*
Grid Reference: *SE 008 062*
Distance: *7.3km/4.5 miles*
Ascent: *280 metres/918 feet*
Time: *2.5 hours*
OS Map: *Explorer OL1: The Dark Peak*

Introduction

Starting at the eighteenth century Cross Keys Inn, above Uppermill, this classic ridgeline traverse offers virtually uninterrupted breathtaking views throughout its course and visits one of Saddleworth's most recognisable landmarks in this 'lost' corner of Yorkshire's ancient West Riding.

Route in Brief

Cross Keys Inn – Running Hill Pits – Broadstone Hill – Slade Rocks – Alderman – Pots & Pans – Pobgreen – Cross Keys Inn

Route Description

This high level ridgeline walk, which offers a wealth of panoramic views, starts from the Cross Keys Inn, which was built in 1745 and situated on the old Marsden Packhorse route. It opened as a tavern in 1763 and still retains many of its original features and character. In addition to being a popular country pub, it is the home of the Oldham Mountain Rescue Team and Saddleworth Runners Club.

Leaving the pub car park, turn left onto Running Hill Gate and follow the lane for approximately 700m. At a sharp left-hand bend, continue straight ahead over a stile, adjacent to a gate, and ascend the sunken walled lane towards Running Hill Pits. The field to the right is used by the Uppermill Clay Pigeon Shooting Club, whose members meet for regular Sunday morning shoots. At the top of the lane, beyond a gate, keep the quarries to your right and follow a faint path to an old stone ruin, which was built in 1836, at the western end of the Cotton Famine Road.

Heading generally south, follow a faint footpath which leads to the upper edge of a quarry. This group of quarries, collectively known as Running Hill Pits, is a

popular playground for climbers. From the quarry rim, the path becomes more obvious and leads directly to the trig point on Broadstone Hill.

Broadstone trig point, first erected by the Ordnance Survey in 1948, marks the start of the traverse of the ridge line over to Alderman's Hill. The trig point was knocked down by vandals in March 1998 and, inspired by a local hill-walker and fell-runner called Frank Sykes, was rebuilt by members of Saddleworth Runners Club on Remembrance Sunday of the same year. Some Ordnance Survey maps actually show the trig point as being named 'Sykes Pillar'. A commemorative plaque to the memory of Frank Sykes - one of the founding members of Saddleworth Runners Club - is located on nearby rocks. Every year on Remembrance Sunday, after attending the remembrance parade at the Saddleworth War Memorial, the members of Saddleworth Runner's Club hold a run over to Syke's Pillar and conduct their own service of remembrance for absent friends.

From the trig point, follow the obvious path across the moor in a generally southerly direction, until you reach a wall corner. The path now continues along the top of the ridge, passing a rocky outcrop on the right called Slade Rocks. Beyond here is a large lone boulder, known locally as the Sugar Loaf. A little further on, the route crosses a prominent 4x4 track and continues over Dick Hill, before descending into a saddle, prior to the grassy climb up onto Alderman's Hill.

Up on Alderman, if the weather is fair, take time for a brief stop to enjoy what is arguably the finest vista in Saddleworth. The view from here takes in the Chew Valley skyline and surrounding hills, with the valley and its three reservoirs - Greenfield, Yeoman Hey and Dove Stone - nestled below.

Local legend has it that the boulder-strewn flanks of Alderman Hill and Alphin Pike, which sits across the valley to the south-west, were the homes of two giants named Alderman and Alphin. It is said that the two giants were at first friends, until they both fell in love with a beautiful water nymph, called Rimmon, who resided in the bubbling waters of Chew Brook, in the deep valley below. Alphin eventually won the affections of Rimmon, which caused Alderman to slump into a state of jealousy. After a period of quarrelling, the two giants engaged in mortal combat, throwing giant boulders at each other across the valley. The boulders, which scatter the faces of these two hills, are said to be the result of their battle. Eventually Alphin was struck by a deadly blow and died where he fell. Devastated at the death of her beloved, it is said that Rimmon jumped to her death from the crags above Chew Valley. According to the legend, Rimmon was buried with her lover somewhere upon the slopes of Alphin Pike.

With your back to the valley, and facing the direction from which you came, bear left and descend the grassy hill, in a north-westerly direction, towards the war memorial at Pots & Pans. On approaching the obelisk, follow the path, which climbs out of the re-entrant, and pass through the old wrought iron railings which surround the cenotaph

The war memorial, which commemorates those men of Saddleworth who fought and died in the two world wars, was designed by architect Gilbert Howcroft, who himself fought in the First World War. Unusually, the monument bears the dates 1914 to 1919. The reason for this is that, whilst the Armistice was signed on 11th November 1918, it only marked a temporary cessation of hostilities and it wasn't until the signing of the Peace Treaty of Versailles, on 28th June 1919, that the Great War officially came to an end and the country's service men could finally return home. Every Remembrance Sunday, hundreds of local people, including a full brass band, climb the 1,400ft hill to pay their respects to the country's fallen.

To the south of the cenotaph is a large rock, known locally as Pots & Pans Rock. On top of this gritstone rock are several holes, known as the 'pots & pans', which have formed over thousands of years of weather erosion. Also known as the Druid Stones, it is believed that it was a place of druid worship. In times gone by, people believed that the water found in the 'bowls' had healing properties and was good for curing eye problems.

Before continuing, why not take a seat on the bench located in front of the obelisk and cast your eyes across the villages of Saddleworth below?

From the front of the war memorial, overlooking Greenfield, take the path on the right to the corner of the iron railings. Trending northwards, continue above two small quarries before making the grassy descent to some rough open fields, surrounded by broken walls. Crossing the fields, pass through two stone gateposts and, after veering left, follow the course of a broken wall as it descends the hill to Pobgreen. Upon reaching a fence, turn left and cross a rickety wooden stile, adjacent to the gable-end of a white cottage. Continuing straight ahead, descend a rough sunken path which meets Pobgreen Lane and turn left for the final few metres back to the Cross Keys Inn, where a refreshing pint and some delicious home-cooked food can be enjoyed.

NORTH

THREE RESERVOIRS

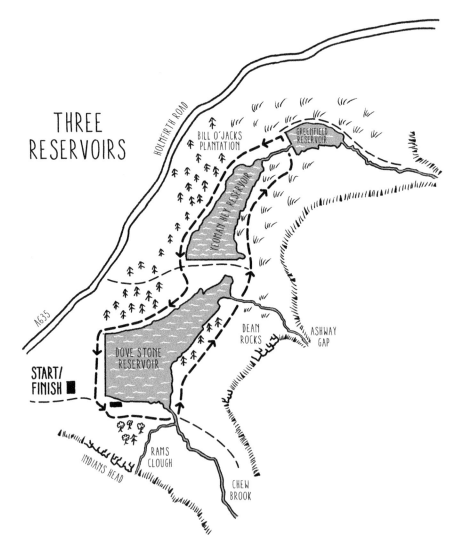

HOLMFIRTH ROAD

BILL O'JACKS
PLANTATION

GREENFIELD
RESERVOIR

YEOMAN HEY RESERVOIR

A635

DEAN
ROCKS

ASHWAY
GAP

DOVE STONE
RESERVOIR

START/
FINISH ■

INDIANS HEAD

RAMS
CLOUGH

CHEW
BROOK

The Three Reservoirs walk

Start/Finish: *Dove Stone car park, Bank Lane, Greenfield*
Grid Reference: *SD 013 035*
Distance: *6.4km/3.9 miles*
Ascent: *70 metres/229 feet*
Time: *2 hours*
OS Map: *Explorer OL1: The Dark Peak*

Introduction

Situated on the outskirts of Oldham, Dove Stone is considered to be the northern gateway to the Peak District National Park. With easy access by both private and public transport, it is very popular with visitors. Its extensive network of footpaths, which provide good links to the open moors, makes it a very popular starting point for hill-walkers and ramblers.

This is an easy walk that offers picturesque views of a constantly changing landscape, which is suitable for families or those not wanting to venture onto higher ground.

Route in brief

Dove Stone Car Park – Chew Brook – Yeoman Hey Reservoir – Greenfield Reservoir – Dove Stone Reservoir – Car Park.

Route Description

From the southern end of the car park, take the tarmac road east, past the sailing club, before passing through a metal kissing gate. Beyond the Field of Remembrance, cross the bridge which spans Chew Brook and follow the path for the short climb to the eastern side of the reservoir.

Dove Stone Reservoir was built in 1967 to collect and supply drinking water for some of the towns which lie on the outskirts of Manchester. It is believed that the reservoir was named after a collection of rocks on the skyline known as Dove Stone which resembles the shape of a dove. However, as there are several sites in the area with similar names, it is thought that the word 'Dove' could have derived from the Celtic word 'dubh', which means black. At the time when the Ordnance Survey was first collating and recording information in the area, the word dubh was still used in local dialect and therefore could have been mistakenly documented as Dove?

Continue along the well-maintained path, which runs along the reservoir's entire length, until reaching its northern end at Ashway Gap. Close to here is the site of a former Victorian hunting lodge called Ashway Gap House. Built in 1777, the majestic, castle-like building was owned by the wealthy Platt family. During the First World War, it was used as a military hospital, and in World War Two as a holding centre for Italian internees, before later becoming a Prisoner of War site. The property was sadly demolished in August 1981, after plans to turn it into an Outdoor Pursuits Centre failed. The layout of the site can still be seen today amongst the rhododendron bushes.

Keeping to the right of the dam wall and overflow steps, take the narrow, often muddy, footpath straight ahead along the eastern shores of Yeoman Hey Reservoir

to the south-west corner of Greenfield Reservoir. After crossing the dam, look up the valley to where a large tower of split rock, known as the 'Trinacle', can be seen at Raven Stones Rocks.

Heading down the valley, and just before reaching the edge of a plantation, turn left down a steep switch-back track to follow a rough trail along the western edge of Yeoman Hey Reservoir.

Constructed in 1880, this is the oldest of the four reservoirs situated in the Dove Stone and Chew Valley area. At the end of this reservoir, set into the dam wall, is a carved stone to commemorate the visit of the king of Tonga who, whilst in the UK to attend the wedding of Prince Charles and Princess Diana in 1981, visited the area to learn about reservoir design and construction methods.

Continuing straight ahead along the tarmac road, turn left through a gate, and walk along the northern shores of Dove Stone Reservoir, from where Wimberry Rocks can be clearly seen on the valley's southern rim. Popular with climbers, this gritstone outcrop is known locally as Indian's Head because, when viewed from the correct angle, it resembles the head of an Indian chief, complete with headdress, lying prone on the skyline. At the far end of the reservoir, cross the dam wall to complete what is an enjoyable stroll around this beautiful, scenic valley.

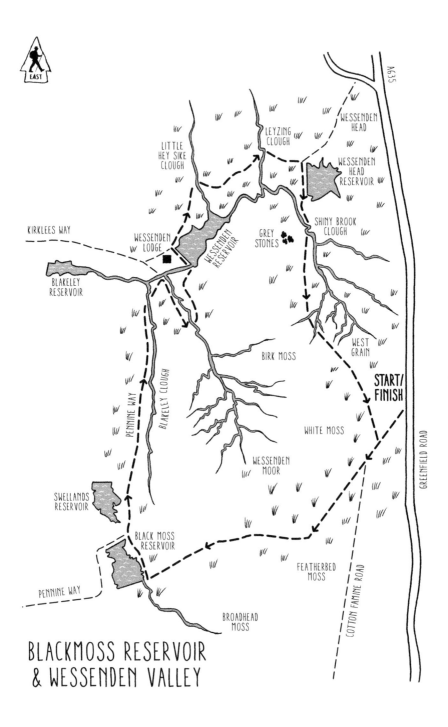

EAST

A635

WESSENDEN
HEAD

LEYZING
CLOUGH

LITTLE
HEY SIKE
CLOUGH

WESSENDEN
HEAD
RESERVOIR

SHINY BROOK
CLOUGH

GREY
STONES

KIRKLEES WAY

WESSENDEN
LODGE

WESSENDEN
RESERVOIR

BLAKELEY
RESERVOIR

WEST
GRAIN

BIRK MOSS

START/
FINISH

PENNINE WAY

BLAKELEY CLOUGH

WHITE MOSS

GREENFIELD ROAD

SWELLANDS
RESERVOIR

WESSENDEN
MOOR

BLACK MOSS
RESERVOIR

PENNINE WAY

FEATHERBED
MOSS

COTTON FAMINE ROAD

BROADHEAD
MOSS

BLACKMOSS RESERVOIR
& WESSENDEN VALLEY

Black Moss Reservoir & Wessenden Valley

Start/Finish: *Old Snoopy's Lay-by. A635, Holmfirth Road*
Grid Reference: *SE 051 063*
Distance: *12km/7.5 miles*
Ascent: *280 metres/918 feet*
Time: *4 hours*
OS Map: *Explorer OL1: The Dark Peak*

Introduction

Setting out along the Pennine Way, this high level moorland walk crosses some rough and exposed terrain. In poor weather conditions, the featureless landscape provides a challenging outing, which is best enjoyed in the company of others.

Route In Brief

Snoopy's Lay-by – Black Moss Reservoir – Wessenden Reservoir – Wessenden Head Reservoir – Shiny Brook Clough – Snoopy's Lay-by

Route Description

This walk sets out from the large unsurfaced layby, known locally as Old Snoopy's, on the A635 Saddleworth to Holmfirth Road. Crossing the stile, follow the original course of the Pennine Way towards Blackmoss Reservoir. This path is now flagged for much of its course with large stone slabs, allowing for easy progress across this very wet and boggy moor. Maintain an eagle eye and you will be sure to see a piece of fossilized bamboo, or similar plant, set into one of the slabs.

In March 1993, when I passed this way with a friend en route to Kirk Yetholme, crossing this moor proved a difficult and arduous task. The route was indistinct and visibility was reduced to only a few metres. Laden with heavy rucksacks and with darkness approaching, we struggled to make forward progress as we battled against relentlessly driving wind and rain to make the sanctuary of Globe Farm, above Diggle. On several occasions we fell, into deep man-eating bogs where, had either of us been alone, we could still be today.

These days the controversial man-made path provides easier going for much of the way to Blackmoss Reservoir. Eventually the stone slabs do end, and the path becomes less obvious as it crosses several peat groughs and deep bogs, which have to be carefully negotiated en route to the south-west corner of the reservoir.

Black Moss Reservoir, which provides water for the Huddersfield canal, is unusually dammed at both ends. Swellands Reservoir, to the east, was built later to provide yet more water for the needy canal system. On 29th November 1810, the recently constructed reservoir burst its banks and six people lost their lives in what was known as the Black Flood.

Heading generally east, along the southern shores of these quiet moorland lagoons, follow the indistinct path until once again the Pennine Way becomes paved and follows the course of Blakely Clough where, at a water tank, it cuts back into another much deeper clough. At the head of this re-entrant, cross the weir and continue round to Wessenden Reservoir.

After crossing the dam, turn right and follow the bridleway along the northern shores of the reservoir. The Wessenden Valley was formed during the last Ice Age, when retreating glaciers carved out the valley. Wessenden Reservoir, built in the 1800s, was the first of the four reservoirs constructed in this pleasant and peaceful valley.

Upon reaching Wessenden Head Reservoir, cross the dam wall and follow the footpath into Shiny Brook Clough. Construction on this upper reservoir started on 27th March 1877 and was completed on 18th August 1881 at a cost of £57,510 5s 5d.

Beyond a weir, the footpath peters out and it is a good idea to make a bid for higher ground. By contouring along the northern slopes of the clough, if enough height is gained, you can avoid climbing in and out of several deep peat groughs which disect the route as they run into West Grain.

Continuing generally south-west along the watershed, from Birk Moss and across White Moss, you will eventually be reunited with the Pennine Way. Turn left now and soon you will arrive back at your start point.

Note

The route across Birk Moss and White Moss to the Pennine Way, can be notoriously wet and is booby-trapped with deep bogs. Care should be taken when crossing this stretch of moor, for one false step could result in a peaty incarceration. In poor visibility, it may be advisable to remain in the sanctuary of Shinny Brook Clough and follow the length of its course into West Grain, which will lead you almost back to Snoopy's lay-by.

DOBCROSS
TRAIL

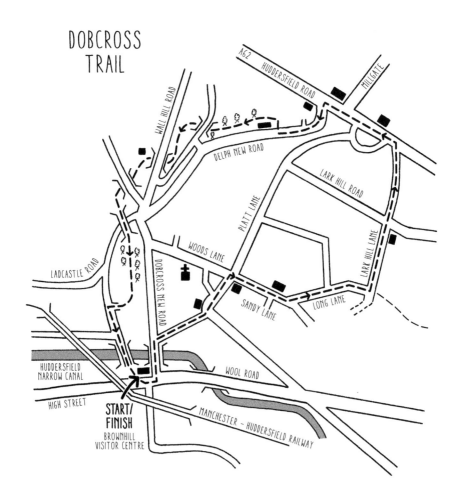

WEST

A62 HUDDERSFIELD ROAD

MILLGATE

WALL HILL ROAD

DELPH NEW ROAD

LARK HILL ROAD

PLATT LANE

LARK HILL LANE

LADCASTLE ROAD

WOODS LANE

DOBCROSS NEW ROAD

SANDY LANE

LONG LANE

HUDDERSFIELD
NARROW CANAL

WOOL ROAD

HIGH STREET

MANCHESTER - HUDDERSFIELD RAILWAY

**START/
FINISH**
BROWNHILL
VISITOR CENTRE

Dobcross Trail

Start/Finish: *Brownhill Countryside Centre, Wool Road, Uppermill*
Grid Reference: *SD 995 063*
Distance: *4km/2.5 miles*
Ascent: *150 metres/492 feet*
Time: *2 hours*
OS Map: *Explorer OL1: The Dark Peak*

Introduction

This easy walk follows quiet country lanes, bridleways and the Delph Donkey Trail as it explores Saddleworth's rich historic past in and around the picturesque village of Dobcross.

Sitting at an ancient crossing point of the River Tame, Dobcross was the centre of the domestic flannel and woollen cloth production industry. Throughout the village and surrounding areas you will see fine examples of many of the original 17th and 18th century weavers' cottages, and the mills that were built to meet the demands of production.

Route in brief

Brownhill Visitor Centre – Dobcross Village – Lark Hill – Huddersfield Road – Delph Donkey – Brownhill Visitor Centre

Route Description

Brownhill Countryside Centre was built in 1916 as stables and used as a transport depot by Saddleworth Urban District Council. In 1982, it became a visitor centre, complete with picnic area and an award-winning nature garden.

Leaving the car park, turn left onto High Street followed by an immediate left onto Dobcross New Road. At the junction, on the opposite side of the road, once stood the Brownhill Bridge Toll House, which eventually became a sweet shop until it was demolished in the 1960s to make way for a road widening scheme. Continuing west, cross the bridge which carried the Oldham & Ripponden Trust turnpike road, and turn immediately right onto Nicker Brow, which is believed to be part of a medieval trading route. On the right is the late 18th century Brownhill Bridge Mill, which was originally used as a teasing mill. In front of the mill, and hidden in the undergrowth, is a medieval packhorse bridge which spans Diggle Brook and was part of an ancient trans-Pennine trading route between Lancashire and Yorkshire.

At the top of Nicker Brow, on Sugar Lane, is Bridge House. Built in the 1790s, it was a master clothier's house and is a surviving example of the village's former thriving woollen industry. The 'takin' in steps' can clearly be seen, up which wool would have been taken for storage. Henry Platt was born here in 1793 and he built Carding Engines in the outbuildings. He went on to form Platt Brothers, which was to become the largest textile machinery manufacturing business in the world.

Continuing on, the Ramsden Memorial can be seen standing in the village square. Erected in 1901, it is dedicated to W.H.F. Ramsden, who was the village doctor from 1864 to 1900. Behind is the old village bank, clear evidence of the village's former commercial standing. A short detour down Woods Lane, which was once the main road to Delph, is Holy Trinity Church. Completed in 1793, it is one of Saddleworth's oldest surviving churches. Its clock was nicknamed the 'Dobcross Lie', because of its unreliable timekeeping.

Returning to the village square, why not enjoy some refreshment in the Swan Inn? Built in 1765, this traditional village pub has a rich history. In the mid-1700s, it was owned by the Wrigley family, some of whom emigrated to America and formed the Wrigley Chewing Gum company. Originally called the Kings Head, it is known locally as the Top House.

Heading north-east along Sandy Lane, pass Sandy Lane Community Church and take the left-hand fork onto Long Lane. Making your way uphill, the route eventually becomes a rough track as it continues its ascent of Lark Hill. At the top of the climb, the view opens out to the north, over to Diggle, and Boat lane can be seen in the distance, climbing past the large spoil heaps created as a result of the excavation of the Standedge tunnels.

Turning left onto Lark Hill Lane, Wharmton Hill, with its needle-like communications mast, dominates the skyline to the south. After crossing Harrop Edge Lane, make the steep descent to the A62 Huddersfield Road, which was the third and final turnpike road to cross the Pennines, at Standedge cutting, to the north-east. The name 'turnpike' derives from the spiked barrier that was placed across the road at the toll-bars.

Turning left, head along Huddersfield Road, towards Delph crossroads, past the Old Bell Inn which is a former 18th century coaching house. In 1835, the then Princess Victoria stayed here with her mother, whilst on their way to the York Festival.

At the crossroads adjacent to the old Delph railway station, which is now a private residence, turn left along New Delph Road. A little further on, behind Station Approach, is Bailey Mill, which stood at the end of the Delph Donkey railway line. Some of the tracks and sidings can still be seen today. It was from here that a tramway extended into the Castleshaw Valley to transport materials during the construction of the two reservoirs.

Continuing along New Delph Road, and upon reaching a slight left-hand bend, just before a row of cottages, cross the road and ascend a set of steps to reach the disused railway line known as the Delph Donkey.

Opened in 1849, it was a branch line of the London and North Western Railway (LNWR) that connected Oldham, Greenfield and Delph to the main Huddersfield to Manchester route. It is believed that early services along the line were horse-drawn, giving the line its name. Passenger services ceased on 30th April 1955, although a limited freight service continued. In 1960, the Royal Train, carrying the Queen Mother, pulled into Delph station for a quiet overnight halt. The line finally closed on 4th November 1963 and is now the Delph Donkey Trail, which is popular with walkers, cyclists and horse riders. Lined with several species of trees, and with a variety of wildflowers growing along the embankments, the trail is recognised as an important biodiversity corridor.

Heading south along this leafy trail, a notice board is soon reached which provides information about the small, unmanned station that served the Measurements Factory. Demolished in the late 1980s, the factory produced precision clocks and instruments.

A little further on, the trail passes underneath Wall Hill Road. Formerly spelt 'Wauhill', the name is of Saxon origin meaning 'Wellhill', which is probably associated with the many wells and springs scattered around the area. At the bottom of the road is a small stream that is reputed to have once been known for the purity of its water.

On the right, immediately beyond the road arch, over which runs Wall Hill Road, stands one of the only remaining buildings of Bankfield Mill. Built in 1858, the mill produced woollen cloth until it was destroyed by fire in the 1940s. The local poet and writer, Ammon Wrigley, worked at the mill from around 1883 until 1932. Beyond the nearby Streethouse Lane bridge, upon the site of the present Ladcastle Mews, stood Tambridge Mill.

Continuing further on, you will come to the site of Dobcross Halt. Originally opened in 1912, this small station was built of wood and was accessed from Ladcastle Road by a set of stone steps, which are still in existence today.

With the walk nearing its end, continue until, just beyond a final horse-stile, a fingerpost directs the way to Uppermill and Brownhill Countryside Centre. Turning left along Mow Lane, pass underneath the arched bridge, which the Delph Donkey line would have crossed, to meet the main Manchester to Huddersfield route. When the Uppermill viaduct comes into view, fork left down a short track to the Huddersfield Narrow Canal. After crossing the stone bridge, at Lime Kiln Lock, turn left to return to the Brownhill Visitor Centre.

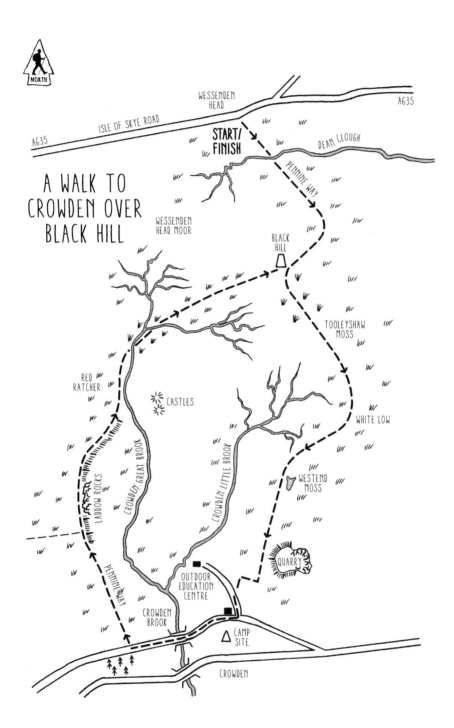

NORTH

WESSENDEN
HEAD

A635

ISLE OF SKYE ROAD

A635

START/
FINISH

DEAN CLOUGH

PENNINE WAY

A WALK TO
CROWDEN OVER
BLACK HILL

WESSENDEN
HEAD MOOR

BLACK
HILL

TOOLEYSHAW
MOSS

RED
RATCHER

CASTLES

WHITE LOW

LADDOW ROCKS

CROWDEN GREAT BROOK

CROWDEN LITTLE BROOK

WESTEND
MOSS

QUARRY

PENNINE WAY

OUTDOOR
EDUCATION
CENTRE

CROWDEN
BROOK

CAMP
SITE

CROWDEN

A walk to Crowden over Black Hill

Start: *Wessenden Head, A635, Saddleworth/Holmfirth Road*
Grid Reference: *SE 075 072*
Distance: *19.4 km/12 miles*
Ascent: *768 metres/2,519 feet*
Time: *6 hours*
Map: *Explorer OL1: The Dark Peak*

Introduction

Setting out along the Pennine Way, the route climbs to the barren summit of Black Hill, which is the highest point in West Yorkshire. Crossing Tooleyshaw Moss, you will continue south over White Low before descending Hey Moss into Crowden, which is the first overnight stop for many Pennine Way walkers heading north from Edale. Until the construction of the five reservoirs which lie in the valley of Longdendale, Crowden was a thriving village, situated on a Middle Ages trans-Pennine packhorse trail or 'saltway'.

From Crowden, the route turns to the north and once again follows the Pennine Way as it makes its way over Laddow Rocks to return to the summit of Black Hill for the final leg back to Wessenden Head.

Route in Brief

Wessenden Head – Black Hill – Tooleyshaw Moss – Westend Moss – Crowden Brook Bridge – Laddow Rocks – Crowden Great Brook – Black Hill – Wessenden Head

Route Description

This walk of approximately 12 miles with around 2,500 feet of ascent starts from the lay-by on the A635 at Wessenden Head. This section of road is known locally as the Isle of Skye Road, and many people believe that its name derives from the name of the public house that stood here until it was demolished in the 1950s, following a terrible fire. However, Bob Tait, in his book Saddleworth Days, states that it could in fact originate from the ancient Norse word 'skyre' which means 'scar or 'ridge'. Another suggestion is that the name could have been adopted after a local man informed a wandering traveller, "Tis arl sky up theer". Whatever its origins, there is no doubt that this vast expense of moorland surely is 'Big Sky Country'.

Setting out from Wessenden Head, follow the paved footpath which descends the moor to Dean Clough before continuing the long ascent to the trig point on the summit of Black Hill.

At 1,908 feet (582m), the summit of Black Hill is a vast, black peaty plateau which has little vegetation growing upon it, giving the hill its name. The summit

trig point is known as 'Soldiers Lump', because it was used as a triangulation point by a Royal Engineers survey party conducting the first full mapping survey of Great Britain, between 1783 and 1853. It is said that an examination of the area uncovered the original wooden timbers constructed to support the Ramsden Theodolite which was used in the original Ordnance Survey, known as the Principal Triangulation of Great Britain, or simply the 'Full Survey'.

Leaving the trig point, in a south-easterly direction, and after crossing approximately 300 metres of energy-sapping peat bogs, a fence is reached. Crossing a stile, about 30 metres to the right of a gate, and on the same bearing, aim for a large cairn, complete with wooden post, on Tooleyshaw Moss. To the east of Tooleyshaw Moss stands the 750ft (228m) Holme Moss Transmitting Station which was, at the time of going into service, the BBC's third public transmitter.

Following a series of smaller cairns, the path passes several old grouse butts as it descends Tooleyshaw Moor into an obvious saddle. A short climb brings you

to the plateau of White Low where, heading south-west, the path skirts a little tarn on Westend Moss. From here, the northern edges of Bleaklow can be seen dominating the skyline, stimulating the mind into planning future forays across this bleak wilderness.

Continuing south-west, the path descends the western flanks of Hey Moss to where it joins up with a track coming in from Crowden Little Brook to the north. Follow this track below Loftend Quarry and descend a rocky footpath to a wooden stile. Leaving open country, turn right and head for a wooden ladder stile in the corner of the field. Turn left along the lane and at the entrance to the campsite turn right towards Crowden Brook Bridge.

The campsite was built on the site of the old 17th century Crowden Hall, which was demolished in 1937 by the Manchester Waterworks Company. Beyond the bridge, the track begins to climb and eventually a signpost indicates the direction to take for the Pennine Way. Turn right here and climb over a ladder stile, opposite a small plantation, to follow the Pennine Way along the western flanks of the valley. Heading generally north, you may well encounter numerous heavily laden walkers, who are in the early stages of their quest to reach Kirk Yetholme, over 200 miles away beyond the Scottish border, at the end of Britain's first National Trail.

The footpath gradually ascends the valley side, crossing several streams, including the delightful Oakenclough Brook, on its route to Laddow Rocks. These gritstone rocks, which were very popular in the early days of gritstone climbing, long before Stanage and Froggart became the Mecca for climbing in the Peak District, now seem to have fallen out of fashion. Haunted by ghosts, they are now quiet and seldom visited.

A serious climbing accident at Laddow Rocks in 1928, led to the formation of 'The Joint Stretcher Committee', in 1932, which was to be an instrumental move towards the formation of official Mountain Rescue Teams in Great Britain.

Soon the well-worn path narrows and starts to descend to the valley floor. Upon the valley's eastern flanks the prominent twin rocky outcrops of the 'Castles' defend the head of this wild, picturesque gorge. At the bottom of the descent, the path, often boggy in places, follows Crowden Great Brook upstream, crossing it on occasion, before gradually ascending to Dun Hill, where it climbs the now flagged path to return to the summit of Black Hill.

After once again returning to the trig point, descend the Pennine Way, along which you climbed at the start of the route, to return to the road at Wessenden Head.

NORTH

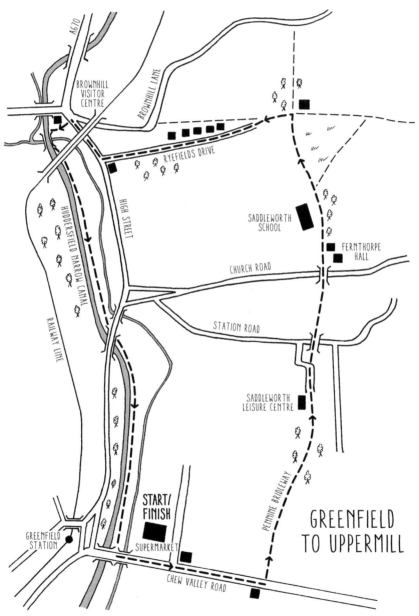

A670

BROWNHILL LANE

BROWNHILL
VISITOR
CENTRE

RYEFIELDS DRIVE

HIGH STREET

HUDDERSFIELD NARROW CANAL

RAILWAY LINE

SADDLEWORTH
SCHOOL

FERNTHORPE
HALL

CHURCH ROAD

STATION ROAD

SADDLEWORTH
LEISURE CENTRE

PENNINE BRIDLEWAY

START/
FINISH

GREENFIELD
STATION

SUPERMARKET

CHEW VALLEY ROAD

GREENFIELD
TO UPPERMILL

Greenfield to Uppermill

Start: *Chew Valley Road, Greenfield*
Grid Reference: *SD 993 045*
Distance: *4.4km/3 miles*
Ascent: *80 metres/262 feet*
Time: *1.5 hours*
OS Map: *Explorer OL1: The Dark Peak*

Introduction

This flat, easy to follow route sets out from Greenfield along the course of an old railway, called the Micklehurst Loop Line. At Ryefields, the route turns south and returns via Uppermill, along one of the most picturesque sections of the Huddersfield Narrow Canal. A low-level walk, it is ideal for bad weather conditions, summer evening strolls or walking off your Sunday lunch.

Route in brief

Greenfield – Pennine Bridleway – Ryefields – Brown Hill Visitor Centre – Huddersfield Narrow Canal – Uppermill – Greenfield

Route Description

Located at the foot of the beautiful Chew Valley and surrounded by dramatic hills, Greenfield has a rich and characterful history. Starting from the front of Tesco supermarket, which stands on the site of an old, historic steam-powered cotton mill, head along Chew Valley Road, past the old Toll House which stands at the junction of Wellington Road. Built some time around 1827, it was in use until Chew Valley Road ceased to be a turnpike road in 1885.

Immediately beyond Greenfield Conservative Club, a signpost directs the way left along the Pennine Bridleway. Approved in 1995 as a designated National Trail, this particular section of the Pennine Bridleway follows the course of a dismantled railway line through Greenfield to Ryefields in Uppermill. The Micklehurst Loop Line, which was mainly used to carry cargo, was 6¾ miles long and ran from Stalybridge to Diggle.

Crossing Higher Arthurs, the route continues past Saddleworth Pool & Leisure Centre before crossing Station Road via a wooden footbridge. Uppermill Station and goods yard was located here and covered an extensive area between what is now Rush Hill Road and Smithy Lane. Some of the original buildings can still be seen today.

A little further on, another wooden bridge crosses Church Road which, when it was reconstructed, had to be built at a height that would still allow the annual Rushcart Procession to proceed underneath, to St. Chad's Church.

The Rushcart is a two-wheeled wooden cart, laden with 3 tonnes of freshly cut rushes stacked 13 feet high. The actual origins of the Rushcart are not certain, however, the pulling of the cart is an old local tradition that evolved from the carrying of rushes to place on the earth floors of churches to act as insulation throughout the cold winter months. In Saddleworth, rushes were originally taken to church on a large sledge. However, this practice eventually evolved into stacking the rushes on top of a cart, forming the shape of a large haystack.

Today the pulling of the Rushcart is an annual festival performed by over 150 Morris Men. Organised by the Saddleworth Morris Men, the Saddleworth 'Longwood Thump' Rushcart ceremony is held every August, when the cart is pulled through the villages of Saddleworth, culminating at St. Chad's Church. Here the rushes are symbolically laid amongst the pews after being mixed with flowers and herbs. After the ceremony, there are displays of traditional Morris dancing, clog-stepping, gurning (face-pulling) and Yorkshire Longsword dancing.

Continuing along the bridleway, Fernthorpe Hall can be glimpsed through the trees. Built in 1869, the present Lord of the Manor, Tony Greene, Esq., a well-known and respected member of the community, has organised and held an annual charity fell race from here known as the Fernthorpe Frolic. With no set route, runners follow their own, closely guarded, lines between the Pots & Pans war memorial on the eastern slopes of the valley and Wharmton to the west, before returning to Fernthorpe Hall for an evening of merrymaking.

At the rear of Saddleworth School, the track splits and the lower, left-hand fork should be taken to Ryefields, where the railway passed through the 329 yard Butterhouse Tunnel (or Ryefield Tunnel) on its final leg to Diggle.

At Ryefields Drive, turn left and walk along the private road to the former Toll House at the junction with High Street. Turning right, walk along High Street to the Brownhill Countryside Centre on Wool Road. Opened in 1982 as a visitor and

information centre, it now hosts the Lime Kiln Café, where a range of meals, drinks and homemade cakes are served.

Leaving the centre, head south along the towpath of the Huddersfield Narrow Canal. Running between Huddersfield and Ashton-under-Lyne, construction of the 20 mile canal began in 1794 but, following a succession of problems, was not completed until 1811. With a total of 74 locks, the canal crosses the Pennines through a tunnel at Standedge, making it the highest navigable waterway in Britain.

A short distance ahead, at Lime Kiln Lock (23w), the canal passes over the River Tame via Saddleworth Aqueduct which, because of its noticeable droop, is known as 'Old Sag'. Overhead is the Saddleworth railway viaduct with its unusual skew arch.

As you walk along the towpath, a variety of water birds can be seen including mallard, heron, geese and moorhen. If you're really lucky, you may even see the shy and elusive kingfisher. Further on, a set of stepping stones lead across the River Tame and provide an opportunity to visit Uppermill village centre, with its array of bars, cafés and shops.

Returning to the canal, continue south to the picturesque Moorgate Street Bridge, where the footpath crosses to the opposite side of the canal and continues its course towards the scenic moorings adjacent to the Saddleworth Museum and Art Gallery. Established in 1962 to preserve the history of the area, the independently operated museum tells the story of the people who have created Saddleworth's diverse landscape and character. Throughout the summer months, regular canal boat trips operate from here, affording people the opportunity to experience what it was like to travel on the canal system over 200 years ago.

Beyond Wade Lock (21w), cross the High Street Bridge and regain the canal towpath via a set of steps. Soon, the heather-clad flanks of Noonsun Hill and Alphin Pike become visible as you pass Churchill Playing Fields on the far bank of the River Tame.

Further on is the newly opened Frenches Marina in which, during the summer months, you can admire many lovingly restored narrowboats berthed at their moorings. Crossing the lifting bridge, make your way past the Kingfisher public house and climb the steps at New Bridge to return into Greenfield along the Chew Valley Road.

EAST

CROSSING
THE BORDER

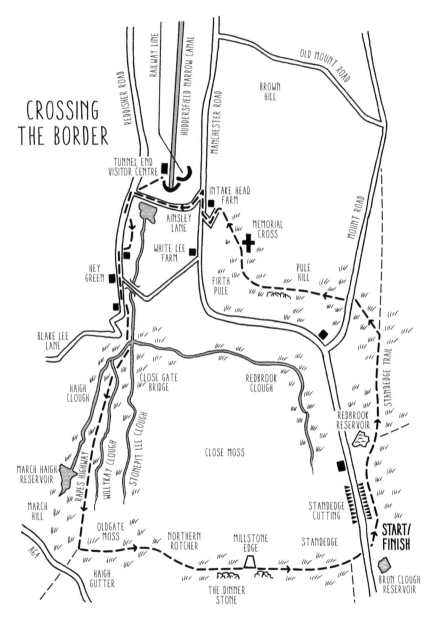

REDDISHER ROAD

RAILWAY LINE

HUDDERSFIELD NARROW CANAL

MANCHESTER ROAD

OLD MOUNT ROAD

BROWN HILL

TUNNEL END VISITOR CENTRE

INTAKE HEAD FARM

AINSLEY LANE

MEMORIAL CROSS

WHITE LEE FARM

PULE HILL

HEY GREEN

FIRTH PULE

MOUNT ROAD

BLAKE LEE LANE

STANDEDGE TRAIL

HAIGH CLOUGH

CLOSE GATE BRIDGE

REDBROOK CLOUGH

MARCH HAIGH RESERVOIR

RAPES HIGHWAY

WILLYKAY CLOUGH

STONEPIT LEE CLOUGH

REDBROOK RESERVOIR

CLOSE MOSS

MARCH HILL

OLDGATE MOSS

NORTHERN ROTCHER

MILLSTONE EDGE

STANDEDGE CUTTING

STANDEDGE

START/ FINISH

A64

HAIGH GUTTER

THE DINNER STONE

BRUN CLOUGH RESERVOIR

Crossing the border: A journey of discovery

Start: *Standedge Cutting car park, A62, Huddersfield Road.*
Grid Reference: *SD 019 095*
Distance: *12.5km/7.8 miles*
Ascent: *730 metres/2,395 feet*
Time: *4.5 hours*
OS Maps: *Explorer OL1: The Dark Peak and OL21: South Pennines*

Introduction

This scenic walk explores the area around the border of the former West Riding of Yorkshire around Standedge and the upper reaches of the Colne Valley, which has been an important trans-Pennine transportation crossing for thousands of years. You will witness evidence of continuous periods of human activity from the Neolithic era to the Bronze Age and through the Roman occupation of Britain to the Industrial Revolution.

The route follows well-defined moorland paths, ancient packhorse routes and a short section of the Pennine Way. In addition to discovering the various transport links and aspects of industrial heritage, you may see a variety of moorland wildlife, including hares, stoats, grouse, curlew, short-eared owl and merlin. In addition, you can find plants such as the crowberry, bilberry and the insect-devouring sundew.

Route in brief

Standedge Cutting – Warcock Hill – Pule Hill – Tunnel End – Close Gate Bridge – Little Moss – Millstone Edge – Standedge Cutting.

Route Description

Standedge is a bleak moorland escarpment which marks the present boundary between Greater Manchester and West Yorkshire and has served as a major moorland crossing point since before Roman times. The earliest recorded highway across the moor is the Roman military road which ran from Chester to York. Thought to have been built around AD80, it was approximately 20 feet wide and, after passing the fort at Castleshaw, crossed Standedge before making its descent towards what is now Marsden.

Providing the narrowest crossing point over the Pennines, Standedge has been identified by generations of engineers as an ideal location for both surface and sub-surface thoroughfares, the best known of which is the Standedge Canal Tunnel.

Leaving the car park via a set of steps, follow the rough path, which parallels the A62 into West Yorkshire, before turning south-east, where it makes a gentle descent

across the moor. Forming part of the Standedge Trail, the course of this old packhorse route was rebuilt as a turnpike road by John Metcalf in around 1791. Known as 'Blind Jack', he was a professional road builder from Knaresborough who between, 1765 and 1792, built a series of toll roads, mainly throughout the north of England. Leading the way in his trade, he devised an effective method of constructing roads across wet moorland, which other engineers believed was impossible. He laid down a line of rafts made from heather and gorse, to form foundations upon which the road was built.

At the bottom of the descent, adjacent to a stone marker, the path dips to the left in order to bypass a section of the turnpike which has collapsed. After crossing the stream, rejoin the track and continue straight ahead over the rise at Warcock Hill. Soon after beginning your descent, leave the turnpike road and follow a narrow footpath on the left which handrails a stream leading to Mount Road. Part of this modern highway follows the course of the first turnpike road that was built to cross Standedge in the mid-1700s.

Crossing the road, climb the steep and well-defined path to the summit of Pule Hill, from which far-reaching views can be enjoyed throughout the full circle of the compass. Popular with paragliders, this distinctive wedge-shaped hill stands like a solitary sentinel above the village of Marsden. The disused quarries and crags which form the hill's western flanks are a regular haunt for climbers. Some years ago, a small Bronze Age cemetery was discovered here, revealing relics of an ancient past.

Continuing north, follow the path to a rectangular airshaft which offers ventilation for the railway tunnel far below your feet. There are, in fact, three parallel railway tunnels. The first was built in 1848, followed by a second in 1871, which was intended to ease congestion at this busy trans-Pennine subterranean crossing. In 1894, a double bore tunnel was opened, complete with twin tracks. At 3 miles and 60 yards long, it is the fifth longest rail tunnel in Britain. Adjacent to the airshaft stands a wooden cross which honours the conduct of the 7th Battalion, the Duke of Wellington's Regiment, during the Second World War.

From the memorial cross, descend Firth Pule, along the course of a broken wall, to Intake Head Farm, where the Colne Valley Circular Walk passes by. Turning left, follow the farm track to the A62 which, when originally constructed in 1839, was the third and final turnpike road. In more modern times, prior to the opening of the M62 motorway, this was the major route between Leeds and Manchester.

After crossing the road with care, turn right towards Marsden and then left down Ainsley Lane to the former Tunnel End Inn on Waters Road. The driveway on the right leads to the Standedge Tunnel Visitor Centre and is an ideal place to rest awhile and enjoy refreshments in the café, which is situated in Tunnel End Cottages, adjacent to the tunnel mouth.

The former canal warehouse has been converted into a Visitor Centre, which tells the history of the Huddersfield Narrow Canal and the tunnel that passes underneath the Pennines at Standedge. If you're lucky, you may see canal boats emerging from the darkness after their deep underground journey from Diggle. When Britain's canal system was first built, narrowboats were drawn by horses. Because the tunnel was built without a towpath, teams of 'leggers' would propel the boats through the 3 mile tunnel, by lying on the boat's roof and walking their feet along the tunnel walls. Opened in 1811, it is the longest, highest and deepest canal tunnel in Britain.

Returning to Waters Road, head west to where, after a short while, a gate leads to a path that follows the course of the stream, which feeds into Tunnel End Reservoir. The path eventually re-emerges onto the lane just before Lower Hey Green cottages, which were once stables for a former nearby mill.

A little further west, a blue plaque on the right commemorates the Hey Green Generator. Water powered, it was installed around 1890 to provide electricity to Hey Green House, which was owned by Joseph Crowther, a prominent local mill owner.

A little further on is Hey Green House. Take a brief detour along the lane opposite and you will see some of the best surviving examples of tenter posts in the area. Tenter-frames were used to stretch and dry washed cloth in textile production. The term 'on tenterhooks' derives from the metal hooks attached to the frames.

Returning to the route, continue along Blake Lea Lane and, opposite Eastergate Cottage, descend a narrow path which follows the course of a stream to Close Gate Bridge. An ancient packhorse bridge, it is known locally as Eastergate Bridge after Esther Schofield, who was once the keeper of the former Packhorse Inn. In old English, 'gate' means road and, over time, Esther's Gate became known as Eastergate. Close Gate derives its name from 'the road to the cloughs'. The bridge serves as a historic reminder of the many ancient trade routes that criss-crossed this wild and desolate landscape.

After crossing the bridge, bear right and follow the path that almost immediately begins to climb onto the moor above the course of Willykay Clough. Now a designated bridleway, this ancient packhorse road, known as Rapes Highway, was once a major trade route to Rochdale. Stone marker posts inscribed 'PH Road' can still be seen along the original route. The posts were erected by the former Marsden Town Council, in 1908, after a 'right of way' dispute with the moor's previous owner, Sir Joseph Radcliffe, Lord of the Manor of Marsden.

As the route ascends steadily across the moor and higher ground is attained, a backward glance provides views over the village of Marsden below. When the terrain allows, March Haigh Reservoir can be glimpsed to the north. To its west is March Hill, which is one of Britain's primary Mesolithic sites, where archaeologists have discovered a range of flint tools and other artefacts dating back to the period.

Throughout Europe, moorland habitats are extremely rare and whilst, at first glance, the windswept landscape may appear bleak and inhospitable, they are, in fact, rich in life. These South Pennine moors are prime breeding locations for ground-nesting birds such as the golden plover and the tiny twite which, although endangered, are said to breed here successfully. As a result, this moorland landscape has been designated as a Site of Special Scientific Interest (SSSI).

After approximately 3 kilometres, level ground is reached at Little Moss and a left-hand turn should be made to follow the course of the Pennine Way. This well-defined path, Britain's best-known National Trail, first crosses a short section of moorland before arriving at a prominent ridgeline which forms the head of the Castleshaw Valley. Prior to the start of this gritstone edge, adjacent to a stream, a stone way-marker is passed where the Pennine Way converges with the Oldham Way. Continuing south-east, traverse this rocky edge via the Dinner Stone, so called because, in 1851, a group of men from the nearby Horse and Jockey Inn had dinner here. Upon reaching the trig point upon Millstone Edge, and if the weather is fair, why not sit for a while and enjoy the last of the views, for the walk is almost complete?

Continuing south, and after leaving the open moorland, the path crosses some walled fields and emerges onto a rough track via a wooden kissing gate. Turn left and, ignoring the first path on the right, make the short walk back to the car park at Standedge Cutting.

If refreshments are required, the Great Western or the Carriage House, on the Yorkshire side of the border, offer a range of beers and food. The Motorman café, below Pule Hill, also provides value for money meals. If time is still in your favour, both Marsden and the villages of Saddleworth are pleasant locations to visit.

NORTH

WHARMTON HILL

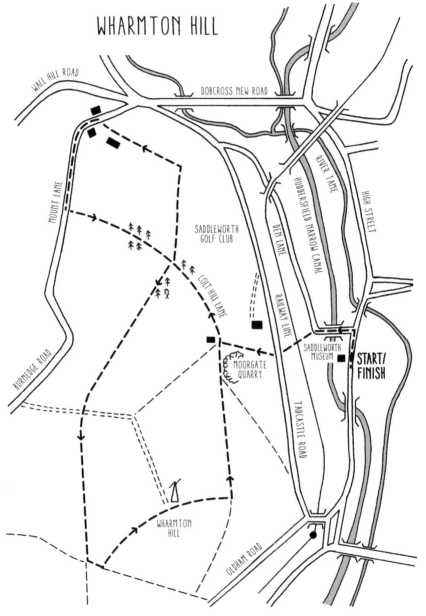

WALL HILL ROAD

DOBCROSS NEW ROAD

RIVER TAME

HUDDERSFIELD NARROW CANAL

HIGH STREET

MOUNT LANE

SADDLEWORTH GOLF CLUB

DEEN LANE

COLT HILL LANE

BURNEDGE ROAD

RAILWAY LINE

MOORGATE QUARRY

SADDLEWORTH MUSEUM

START/ FINISH

TADCASTLE ROAD

WHARMTON HILL

OLDHAM ROAD

Wharmton Hill

Start/Finish: *Saddleworth Museum, Uppermill*
Grid Reference: *SD 996 055*
Distance: *6km/3.7 miles*
Ascent: *350 metres/1,148 feet*
Time: *2 hours*
OS Map: *Explorer OL1: The Dark Peak*

Introduction

This short walk from Uppermill leaves the village via an initial steep climb past Moorgate Quarry, before crossing the immaculately kept greens and fairways of Saddleworth Golf Course. Heading along Streethouse Lane, you will pass the old Wharmton School before crossing the golf course, once again, to leave by its southern boundary. Crossing several fields, the route then traverses the lower flanks of Wharmton before making a final short but steep climb to the summit, from where commanding views of several of Saddleworth's villages are to be enjoyed. The final section makes a gradual descent of the hill back to the upper edges of Moorgate Quarry before returning to Uppermill along the initial outbound route.

Route in brief

Uppermill – Saddleworth Golf Course – Streethouse Lane – Saddleworth Golf Course – Wharmton – Uppermill

Route Description

From Victoria Mill car park, adjacent to the Saddleworth Museum, head along High Street towards the village centre. After a short while, turn left onto Moorgate Street which crosses the Huddersfield Narrow Canal. At Den lane, where the road makes a sharp right-hand bend, take the footpath along Dark lane, which is clearly signposted and leads to the railway line. Taking care, cross the tracks and continue uphill along a leafy footpath known as Dry Clough Lane where, if you're lucky, you may get a glimpse of a green or great spotted woodpecker.

Crossing Ladcastle Road, continue uphill, past Moorgate Quarry which was in use from the late 1800s until it was abandoned in the mid-1970s, allowing nature to reclaim this once industrial site. Covering over seven hectares, the quarry is now designated as a Site of Biological Importance (SBI) and is rich in flora and fauna, supporting a diverse range of wildlife.

At the top of the climb, upon emerging into a field, bear right to a stone step-stile which provides access to Saddleworth Golf Course. Crossing the golf course with care, and giving way to golfers, continue along a track called Colt Hill Lane, until you meet a four-way signpost. Following the signpost for Tame Water, turn right and continue past a small pond where the path follows a fence-line through the long grass. Soon the quaint little village of Dobcross comes into view, nestled at the foot of the solitary Lark Hill.

Reaching the northern boundary of the golf course, cross a stile on the left to follow the course of a stone wall along the edge of a field which in summer is covered in a yellow carpet of buttercups. At the far side of the field, a gate leads onto Streethouse Lane, where you will pass a cluster of cottages on the left. Opposite The Old Vicarage, turn left and walk uphill past the former Wharmton School. Founded in 1729 by Ralph Hawkyard, it was converted into cottages by Henry Scholes in 1888.

Nearing the top of the climb, a large wooden ladder-stile, on the left, which was erected by Ramblers volunteers, provides access to a field. Crossing the lush hay meadow, the path will return you to the golf course, via a stone step-stile.

Formed in 1904 by a group of prominent local men and women, the course offers dramatic views of the surrounding landscape whilst boasting what is probably the highest tee in England, the 8th, at 1,272 feet above sea level.

Heading through the trees, yellow markers point the way across the fairways. After passing between two large, solitary stone gateposts, head along a track which

runs through a small coniferous plantation to return to the four-way signpost. Following the signpost for Burnedge Lane, turn right and, keeping to the right of the trees, follow the intermittent markers uphill along the left-hand edge of the green. Beyond the green, the path leads through some rough ground to reach a stile at a wall corner. Crossing the stile, follow the wall on the right, along the edge of the hay meadow, past the sign erected by the Peak District and Northern Counties Footpaths Preservation Society, which marks footpath number 146 to Tamewater and Dobcross.

A little further on, glance over the wall and you will see the former St. Paul's Church and Vicarage at Scouthead. Standing on the old Wool Road between Lancashire and Yorkshire, the church was consecrated in 1889 and has now been transformed into a conference and exhibition centre.

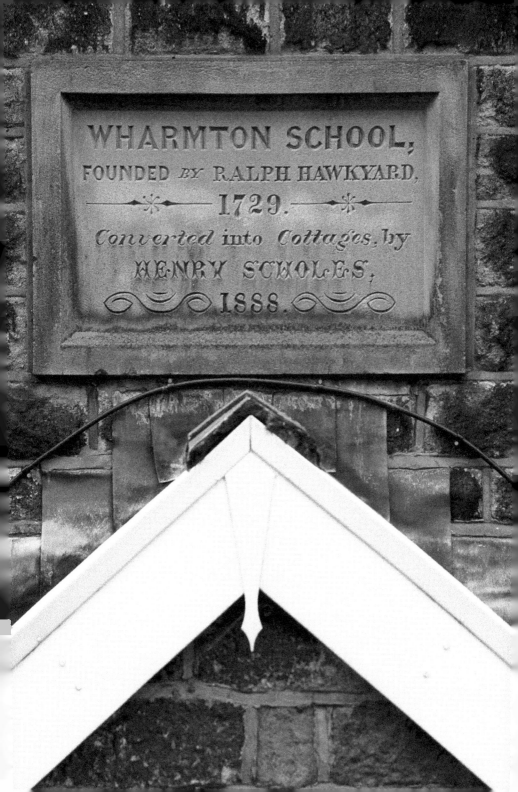

WHARMTON SCHOOL,
FOUNDED BY RALPH HAWKYARD,
1729.
Converted into Cottages, by
HENRY SCHOLES,
1888.

Continuing straight ahead, and soon after crossing another stone step-stile, a track is reached which runs to the summit of Wharmton from Burnedge Lane. At the track cross a wooden stile, directly ahead, and follow a rarely trodden path which parallels a wall across several fields. Upon leaving the fields, make the lung-busting climb up the steep slopes of Wharmton, heading for the mast that can be seen protruding above the skyline. At 1,142 feet, the summit offers extensive views across Saddleworth and beyond.

Skirting round to the eastern side of the compound, head due east and descend the hill for approximately 100 metres before contouring the hillside to return to the upper edge of Moorgate Quarry. Following the outbound route, return to Uppermill, from whence you came.

NORTH

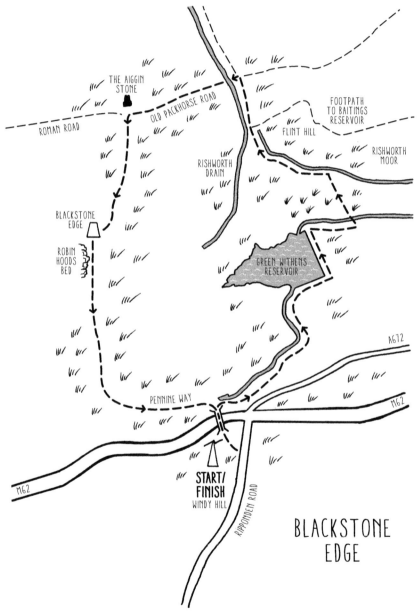

THE AIGGIN
STONE

OLD PACKHORSE ROAD

ROMAN ROAD

FOOTPATH
TO BAITINGS
RESERVOIR

FLINT HILL

RISHWORTH
MOOR

RISHWORTH
DRAIN

BLACKSTONE
EDGE

ROBIN
HOODS
BED

GREEN WITHENS
RESERVOIR

A672

M62

PENNINE WAY

M62

START/
FINISH
WINDY HILL

RIPPONDEN ROAD

BLACKSTONE
EDGE

Blackstone Edge

Start/Finish: *Lay-by A672, Ripponden Road*
Grid Reference: *SD 983 141*
Distance: *10km/6.2 miles*
Ascent: *360 metres/1,181 feet*
Time: *3.5 hours*
OS Map: *Explorer OL21: South Pennines*

Introduction

This classic moorland walk follows distinct paths, tracks and trails across Rishworth Moor before climbing the course of an old packhorse road to an ancient way marker, known as the Aiggin Stone. With the best saved for last, the route makes its way across a great geologically interesting rocky ridge called Blackstone Edge, which marks the ancient border of Lancashire and Yorkshire and provides far-reaching views to both the east and west. An easy descent along a clear path returns you to your start point to the south of the busy, trans-Pennine, M62 motorway.

Route in brief

Rook Stones Hill – Green Withens Reservoir – Rishworth Moor – Aiggin Stone – Blackstone Edge – Rook Stones Hill

Route Description

From the large unsurfaced lay-by on Windy Hill, strike out north along the Pennine Way, which started its 267 mile course in Edale to the south. Keeping the communications mast to your left, continue over the footbridge which crosses the motorway. At 1,221 feet, this is the highest section of the M62 trans-Pennine motorway and the highest point of any motorway in the United Kingdom.

Immediately across the bridge, turn right following the signpost for Green Withens Reservoir. At a water intake pond, a grassy path runs north along the course of a water catchment drain and eventually merges with the reservoir access road, which runs generally north.

Green Withens Reservoir was completed in 1898 to provide water for the Wakefield Corporation Waterworks, and is now owned and managed by Yorkshire Water. It is also used as a water activity centre by the West Yorkshire Scouts.

On approaching the activity centre, the track bears right through a stone wall and continues along the eastern edge of the reservoir. At the northern end of the dam wall stands a small stone building, housing the draw-off valves which control the water outflow. Keeping the building to the left, follow the track round to the right until a bridge is reached which spans the catchment drain. Following the signpost for Blackstone Edge and Baitings Reservoir, cross the bridge and ascend the narrow, often muddy, footpath to attain another shallow drain. Turning left, this route contours the side of Flint Hill and allows better progress than the alternative wetter, and more indistinct, footpath below. Looking to the west, Blackstone Edge dominates the sky line and provides a teasing view of what is yet to come.

The route eventually meets up with the larger and deeper Rishworth Drain, where a signpost indicates the direction for Baitings Reservoir to the right. Ignoring this option, continue straight ahead along the main track to a wooden gate. Pass through the gate and continue approximately 200m to where a wooden bridge spans the drain. Cross the bridge and, passing a stainless-steel rain gauge sunk into the ground, strike out along an indistinct path which parallels an obvious marshy depression on the left. According to the map, this is the course of an old packhorse road. On glancing right, Stoodley Pike can be seen peeking over the distant sky line to the north.

Reaching the top of the climb, the way becomes more distinct and a well-preserved section of what is believed to be a Roman Road eventually becomes evident underfoot. Just beyond the road's highest point stands the Aiggin Stone, which is an ancient way-stone used by medieval travellers crossing the moor between Littleborough and Ripponden. A Latin-style cross is carved into the 4ft high gritstone pillar with the letters 'IT' inscribed below. Some historians think that they may stand for IN TEDIUM, which translates as 'In the Lord we trust' or 'In praise of the Lord'. It is thought that the Aiggin Stone, and similar marker stones found in the area, could have had religious significance. One theory is that coffins could have been rested next to the stone for a while, and prayers for the dead recited. Travellers

may have also stopped to say prayers and make offerings in return for safe passage across these wild, windswept moors.

Where the Roman Road continues on its course down towards the ancient settlement of Littleborough, turn south and cross a wooden stile to follow an obvious rocky path back along the Pennine Way. A few small cairns and some small wooden marker posts provide comfort that the correct route is being followed to the brilliant white triangulation pillar which stands at the summit of Blackstone Edge.

Adjacent to the trig point stands an enormous boulder known locally as Robin Hood's Bed. Atop this rock is a curiously carved 'bed' approximately 6ft long by 3ft wide, on which a man can easily lie. According to local legend, this gritstone boulder is where the famous legendary outlaw once slept. Some historians believe that the site could have been used as an ancient grave or tomb, as the old Welsh word 'bedd' means 'a grave or tomb'. Others offer theory that it may have been used as a place of ritual sacrifice.

With your mind filled with thoughts of legendary outlaws and pagan sacrifices, continue southward along this great ridge. Although making way along the bare peat line offers easier progress, it should be avoided so as not to cause further erosion of this fragile environment and bring about increased eastward migration of the ancient peat soil. As the path descends the southern shoulder of Blackstone Edge, a low stone shelter is passed that is often used by walkers to shelter from a biting wind. The route ahead can be clearly seen, and the noise of the commuting traffic along the M62 motorway comes into earshot. A little further on, after crossing two small streams, a gate is reached and the motorway once again comes into view. Pass through the wooden gate and descend the short stony path which leads back to the Pennine Way footbridge. From here on, the route retraces its original course for the last few hundred metres back to the lay-by on Windy Hill.

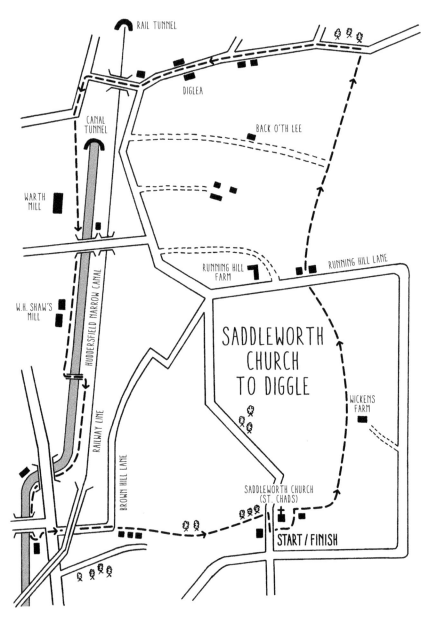

NORTH

RAIL TUNNEL

DIGLEA

CANAL
TUNNEL

BACK O'TH LEE

WARTH
MILL

HUDDERSFIELD NARROW CANAL

RUNNING HILL
FARM

RUNNING HILL LANE

W.H. SHAW'S
MILL

SADDLEWORTH
CHURCH
TO DIGGLE

WICKENS
FARM

RAILWAY LINE

BROWN HILL LANE

SADDLEWORTH CHURCH
(ST. CHADS)

START / FINISH

Saddleworth Church to Diggle

Start: *Saddleworth Church, Church Lane, Uppermill*
Grid Reference: *SE 007 063*
Distance: *7.5km/4.6 miles*
Ascent: *110 metres/360 feet*
Time: *2.5 hours*
Map: *Explorer OL1: The Dark Peak*

Introduction

Starting from St. Chad's Church, which is one of the area's most recognisable landmarks, this mainly flat, low-level route makes an initial foray across farmland to the ancient settlement of Diggle. Here you will see the entrances to both the Standedge rail and canal tunnels, which were spectacular feats of Georgian and Victorian engineering. The return leg follows the course of the Huddersfield Narrow Canal, along which you will see several examples of old mills and canal infrastructure. Upon reaching Brownhill Visitor Centre, a short steady climb over Brown Hill and across Ryefields completes the walk.

Route in brief

Saddleworth Church – Back o'th' Lee – Diggle – Huddersfield Canal – Brownhill Visitor Centre – Saddleworth Church

Route Description

There has been a place of worship upon the site of St. Chad's Church since 1215 AD. According to local legend, the church was originally planned to be built on nearby Brown Hill. However, when building commenced, it is said that every night the stones were mysteriously moved to the present site of the church. Eventually, the builders gave up returning the stones to Brown Hill and built the church where it now stands. The culprits were said to be mischievous fairies who, according to the legend, were banished from Saddleworth when the church first rang its bells. It is also reputed that the church is haunted by a Grey Lady who resides in the grounds.

Ammon Wrigley, the beloved writer of Saddleworth folklore, prose and poems, wrote one of his most famous poems about St. Chad's Church, titled 'Saddleworth Church'.

From the front of the church, adjacent to the old stocks, dated 1698, take the obvious path uphill which handrails the high boundary wall of the graveyard. At the top of the path, bear right through the yard of Clerks Cottage, to a stile on the left beyond an outbuilding. Following the Oldham Way, make your way north across several fields, past Wickens Farm, to Running Hill Lane.

A slight detour down the lane will take you to Running Hill Farm, which for over 120 years was a workhouse. At its peak, the Saddleworth Union Workhouse accommodated 199 inmates, although this number was reduced to around 80 in 1896. Some time after 1930, the workhouse closed and it was for some years used as a geriatric hospital. Later, it became a farm, and the original main workhouse building was demolished. The long, single-storey building to the east of the site, which can be seen clearly from the road, contained a porter's lodge, medical wards and a mortuary. The buildings to the north were formerly a laundry, piggeries, a cowshed and a barn. The site is now a collection of unique residential properties.

Returning back along the lane from where you came, turn left down the narrow footpath between Running Hill Farm House and The Cottage. From here, way-markers indicate the route across several fields to the east of Back o'th' Lee. Soon, a stone arched bridge comes into view in the distance, under which flows Diggle Brook. Eventually, the route bears left and follows a watercourse before making way along a track to emerge onto a private road that accesses the former Diggle Mill. Look closely in the undergrowth and you will find an old stone statue, which guards the entrance to this once prosperous mill which was powered by the second largest waterwheel in the United Kingdom.

Heading west, follow the lane past Marsh Head Farm and through the ancient hamlet of Diglea. Believed to have been occupied since the 13th century, it is the oldest settlement in Diggle. A few yards further on, you will reach the Diggle Hotel. Originally a beer house, it was granted a hotel licence in 1859. Serving fine ales and good food, the pub offers an ideal opportunity for some welcome refreshment.

Continuing straight ahead over the railway bridge, you can see the entrance to the Standedge railway tunnels. The first tunnel was built in 1848, followed by a second in 1871, which was intended to ease congestion at this busy trans-Pennine crossing. In 1894, a third, twin-tracked, tunnel was opened, which remains in use today. At 3 miles, 60 yards long, it is the fifth longest rail tunnel in Britain. A regular service runs between Manchester and Huddersfield, and you will not have to linger long to see a train either entering or emerging from the tunnel mouth.

Turning left, walk down Sam Road and through a car park, which leads onto the towpath of the Huddersfield Narrow Canal, where you will find the western entrance to the Standedge canal tunnel. Opened in 1811, the tunnel took sixteen years to complete at a cost of £123,804, nearly twice the original estimated cost. The first boat to pass through the longest, highest and deepest canal tunnel in Britain, on 4th April 1811, was called the Lively Lady. Canal boats were originally horse-drawn, and with no towpath being built, boats had to be 'legged' through the tunnel by men who lay on the roof of the boat and pushed it along with their feet. The horses were then walked over the hill, via Boat Lane, to be reunited with their vessels on the far side of the Pennines.

Throughout the nineteenth century, the canal system was the main transportation route for goods across the country, and in 1838 as many as thirty narrowboats passed through Standedge Tunnel every day. However, with the building of the railways and improved road systems for the newly developed motorised transport, long-distance transhipment along the waterways diminished. The last working boat passed through the tunnel in November 1921 and commercial navigation was officially ended by an act of Parliament in 1944.

In 1981, members of the Huddersfield Canal Society began restoring the waterway. Eventually, with the aid of a Millennium Lottery Fund grant, and in association with British Waterways and the local authorities, at a cost of over £45 million, the canal and tunnel were officially re-opened by the Prince of Wales in 2001.

Continuing along the towpath, you will pass Warth Mill. Named after a small field, it was originally built in 1780 as a fulling mill, which is a process used in woollen cloth-making. Further on, adjacent to Ward Lane Lock (3lw) is Grandpa Greene's Luxury Ice Cream shop. At weekends during the summer months, you can rest here awhile and enjoy one of their fine home-made ice creams. Crossing the road, continue along the canal past W.H. Shaw's mill, which was originally the Dobcross Loom Works. The elegant main building, with its distinctive clock tower, is known locally as 'The Cathedral'. If you keep a weather eye out, you will notice, to the right of the footpath, iron boundary markers bearing the inscription LNWR. These mark the property line of the land that was owned by the London North-Western Railway Company.

Approximately 1 kilometre further on, just beyond bridge number 71, is the Wool Road Visitor Mooring Area. On the far bank is the old transhipment warehouse, used to transfer goods from the mills. The building now houses the offices of the Canal & River Trust and the Huddersfield Canal Society. Adjacent is an old woollen mill that has now been turned into luxury accommodation.

Crossing a small car park, re-join the water's edge for the short walk to Brownhill Visitor Centre, where you can learn about the local environment and Saddleworth's rich and varied history. After crossing Wool Road, make the short but steep climb up Brownhill Lane, passing underneath Saddleworth Viaduct. With 23 arches, this massive stone structure has carried trains across the valley since 1849.

At the top of the climb, where the lane bends to the left, continue straight ahead along the track past a property called Ryemoor. After a few metres, keep to the right and follow a narrow footpath which passes behind a row of large houses. At the end of the path, turn left along Ryefields Drive and go through an old wrought iron kissing gate into a field, in which there are usually several horses grazing. To the south-west, the Pots & Pans War Memorial can be seen on the skyline. Initially following the course of a broken wall, cross the fields in the direction of the church tower which can be seen above the trees. After crossing a stream, climb the stony path and turn right along Church Lane to return to Saddleworth Church.

With the walk now complete, why not sit by the fire in the Church Inn, where they serve good food and fine ales? You can even sample their range of bespoke beers, brewed on site in their own award-winning microbrewery.

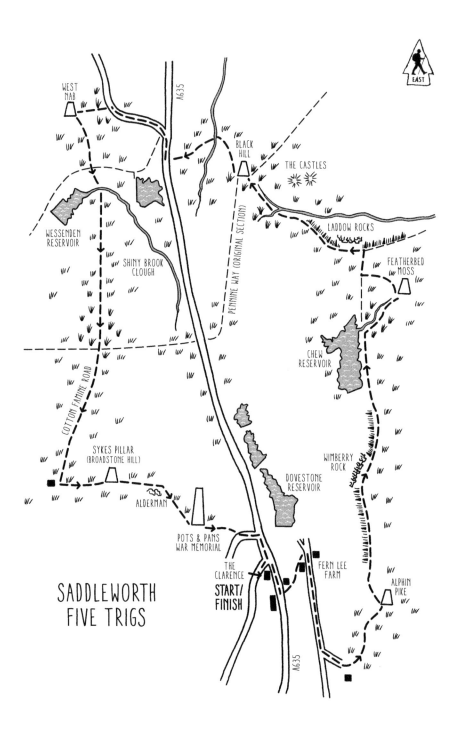

WEST NAB

A635

BLACK HILL

THE CASTLES

LADDOW ROCKS

WESSENDEN RESERVOIR

SHINY BROOK CLOUGH

PENNINE WAY (ORIGINAL SECTION)

FEATHERBED MOSS

CHEW RESERVOIR

COTTON FAMINE ROAD

SYKES PILLAR (BROADSTONE HILL)

ALDERMAN

WIMBERRY ROCK

DOVESTONE RESERVOIR

POTS & PANS WAR MEMORIAL

THE CLARENCE

START/ FINISH

FERN LEE FARM

ALPHIN PIKE

SADDLEWORTH FIVE TRIGS

A635

EAST

Saddleworth Five Trigs

Start: *Clarence Hotel, Greenfield*
Grid Reference: *SD 001 040*
Distance: *32km/19.9 miles*
Ascent: *1,040 metres/3,412 feet*
Time: *8.5 hours*
OS Maps: *Explorer OL1: The Dark Peak*

Introduction

This long-distance walk covers some exposed and remote moorland terrain whilst visiting the trig points on Alphin Pike, Featherbed Moss, Black Hill, West Nab and Broadstones Hill. Originally devised in the early 1970s by Bob Tait, it was later adopted by Oldham Mountain Rescue Team as an annual training walk. Popular with fell-runners and long-distance walkers, the route has been detailed in several books, including Bill Smith's Studmarks on the Summits.

Route in brief

Clarence Hotel – Alphin Pike – Featherbed Moss – Black Hill – West Nab – Broadstone Hill – Clarence Hotel

Route Description

From the Clarence Hotel in Greenfield, head west along the A635 Manchester Road towards Mossley. Just beyond the primary school, opposite a row of cottages, turn left up a grassy track, signposted public footpath. After crossing a stile, ascend the fields to gain Intake Lane via a wooden gate, to the left of Fern Lee Farm. Proceeding west, continue along the lane to White Lee where, on the left, a stony track leads to the ruins of Mount Pleasant Farm. At the top of the lane, turn left and follow the clear path which climbs the shoulder of Alphin Pike to the trig point and shelter on the summit. From this vantage point, far-reaching views are to be enjoyed on a clear day. To the north, the villages of Greenfield and Uppermill lie beneath the Pots & Pans war memorial, whilst to the west sits Oldham, with its Civic Centre breaking the skyline. Over to the south-west are views across Stockport and Manchester which, on a clear night, make for a fantastic spectacle of light. Closer to home, the site of Buckton Castle can be seen above Buckton Vale Quarry.

From the shelter, take the path which runs south-east along Slack Head Brow and crosses the bare peat to Wimberry Rocks. Known locally as Indian's Head, these gritstone crags are a popular playground for climbers.

From here, continue along the precipitous edges past Chew Hurdles to where the jagged gritstone edge mingles into the moorland peat. From this point, the route

becomes a little less obvious as it crosses bare peat on its course to the south-western corner of Chew Reservoir.

Constructed in 1912 at 1,600ft (488m) above sea level, Chew Reservoir was, until 1971, the highest man-made reservoir in England. Standing at the head of the Chew Valley, its waters flow down Chew Brook and into Dove Stone Reservoir below.

Continuing east along the shoreline to where Green Grain flows into the dark waters of the reservoir, turn south and follow the grain's course towards the trig point on Featherbed Moss. This remote area of moorland is very reluctant to allow visitors to lock their eyes onto the concrete triangulation pillar until the very last minute. With that in mind, in conditions of low visibility, accurate navigation will be required to locate this elusive pyramid.

Turning your back on the lonely pillar, head north-east across the moor until the footpath from Chew Reservoir is once again intercepted. At this point turn right along the path until reaching the Pennine Way, making its journey northbound, above Laddow Rocks.

Beyond Laddow Rocks, the route follows a narrow, heavily worn path along the upper edge of the western flank of the valley. Eventually, it makes a gradual

descent to the valley floor and follows Crowden Great Brook, which it crosses on occasions, before climbing the now stone paved path to the summit of Black Hill.

Before the path was laid, the plateau of Black Hill made for a very unpleasant crossing in often knee-deep peat bogs. At 1,908 feet (582m), it is the highest point in the county of West Yorkshire and is one of four summits visited on the Dark Peak Four County Tops route. At 40 miles and with around 7,000ft of ascent, this testing outing visits the highest points in Derbyshire, South Yorkshire, West Yorkshire and Greater Manchester.

From the trig point, continue along the slabs in a north-easterly direction, along the new section of the Pennine Way. After a short while the flag stones do end, but the route soon becomes paved once again as it makes its descent to Dean Clough. After periods of heavy rain, this stream can run in spate and great care should be taken when crossing. Some years ago, on a particularly cold December morning, when I was running in an endurance race from Marsden to Edale called 'Tanky's Trog', this usually calm stream was in flood. Dressed in shorts, I had to stand, waist-deep, in the freezing cold waters for several minutes whilst I helped groups of other runners to cross to the far bank.

Hopefully with your feet still dry, make your ascent to the A635 Saddleworth to Holmfirth Road. At certain times of the day, a mobile catering van can be found parked here and if you time your arrival to coincide with opening hours, refreshments may be obtained to provide much-needed energy for the route to come.

Crossing the Isle of Skye Road, as it is known locally, turn left onto Wessenden Head Road, which leads to Meltham. Beyond the point where the road turns north-east, leave the highway and climb the southern face of West Nab to attain the penultimate trig point, hidden amongst the gritstone rocks.

With the fourth trig point now in the bag, good progress can be enjoyed for a short while on the path that runs along the prominent spur to the west of West Nab. Beyond this spit of high ground, the going becomes rougher underfoot as the tussocky ground that is common in the Wessenden Valley is encountered on the descent of Layzing Clough.

Upon reaching the valley floor, cross Wessenden Brook before making a bid for higher ground to the north of Grey Stones. Heading generally south-west, cross Wessenden Moor, which in the summer months is covered in a blanket of white fluffy cotton-grass, to gain the Cotton Famine Road at Grid: 048 066.

At first glance, the Cotton Famine Road is quite indistinct and looks like nothing more than a wide flat section of ground, flanked on both sides by shallow ditches. If visibility is poor, accurate navigation will be required to locate it.

The Road was said to have been built in the 1860s to alleviate the unemployment of the cotton mill workers, as a result of the Union's blockade of Confederate ports during the American Civil War. However, some historians believe that its construction could have started much earlier. The ditches which flank the central section of road are said to be marked on the 1854 Ordnance Survey map of the area. Some evidence, apparently, suggests that the road's construction may originally have begun around 1811.

Continue along the Cotton Famine Road for approximately 3 kilometres, until an old ruined stone building, built in 1836, is reached at the western end of this unused Victorian labour project. Turning generally south, follow a faint path which skirts the upper edge of a small quarry and leads directly to Broadstones trig point.

With all of the trig points now in the bag, head off in a southerly direction along a clear path passing Slades Rocks, towards Dick Hill. Just beyond a large boulder known as The Sugar Loaf, turn right along a prominent track that descends the western slopes of Dick Hill, to the Pots & Pans War Memorial, which stands in view of Saddleworth's villages.

With the walk nearing its end, continue south, past a large weather-eroded rock known as 'The Pots & Pans', from where a grassy path sweeps through a small quarry before descending to Edge End. Crossing a broken wall, continue straight ahead following the obvious route across several fields to reach Long Lane. Crossing a wooden stile, where a sign informs that dogs must be kept on a leash, descend the footpath which leads to Hawk Yard. Turning right past the front of a stone property, turn left through a gate into a field. Descending the fields, turn left along Tunstead Lane and then right onto Holmfirth Road, to return to the Clarence public house for a well-deserved pint.

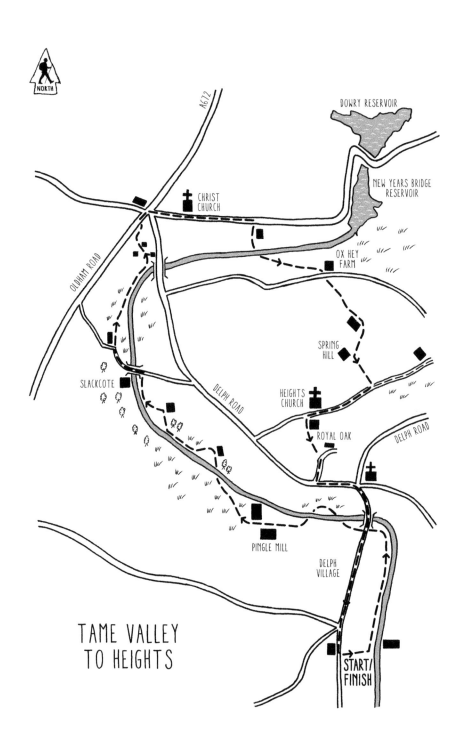

NORTH

A672

DOWRY RESERVOIR

NEW YEARS BRIDGE
RESERVOIR

CHRIST
CHURCH

OX HEY
FARM

OLDHAM ROAD

SPRING
HILL

SLACKCOTE

DELPH ROAD

HEIGHTS
CHURCH

ROYAL OAK

DELPH ROAD

PINGLE MILL

DELPH
VILLAGE

TAME VALLEY
TO HEIGHTS

START/
FINISH

Along the Tame Valley to Heights

Start: *Millgate Car Park, Millgate, Delph*

Grid Reference: *SD 986 078*

Distance: *8.2 kilometres/5 miles*

Ascent: *270 metres/885 feet*

Time: *3 hours*

OS Maps: *Explorer OL1: The Dark Peak and OL21: South Pennines*

Introduction

Starting from the quaint little village of Delph this easy, delightful walk sets out along the Tame Valley, where you will see rich evidence of the area's historic and industrial past. At the head of the valley, you will pass through Denshaw, Saddleworth's most northerly village, which has seen human activity since the Stone Age. Leaving the valley, the route now crosses farmland to the 18th century Heights Chapel, which has appeared in several films and television productions. Here you can enjoy a rest in the Heights Pub before making the final short descent back into Delph.

Route in brief

Delph – Slackote – Denshaw – Ox Hey Farm - Lockwood Hey Farm – Heights – Delph Greave – Delph

Route Description

Nestled at the convergence of the Castleshaw and Denshaw valleys, Delph derives its name from the old English word 'delf', which means 'quarry'. Bakestones were quarried in the Castleshaw Valley, just to the north of the village: the three-quarter inch thick quarried tiles were used to bake oatcakes and muffins. The area was probably first populated around the time that the Roman garrison was stationed at the Castleshaw Fort in AD79. From the late 1700s, the area supported the thriving textile industry, and the centre of the village has changed little since the early 19th century.

The start point for this delightful walk is Millgate car park opposite the Co-operative Hall. Built in 1864, the hall is now a theatre and library and is managed by a local theatrical group called Saddleworth Players.

At the bottom of the car park, adjacent to a house called Well Brow, take the footpath north along the River Tame towards Delph Bridge. Beyond the bridge, on the northern bank of the river, is a stone cottage that bears an Ordnance Survey benchmark which marks the height of the floodwaters that swamped the village on 13th July 1872.

Following the fingerpost, which directs the way to Denshaw, continue along the Tame Valley. Soon the route crosses to the far bank for a short while before once again gaining the south bank via a stone bridge. Passing a children's adventure play park, follow the Tame Valley Way on its course along the valley bottom to Pingle Mill, where textile manufacturing has been carried out since 1777. Now operated by R. Gledhill Ltd, the family-run business, established in 1936, produces high-quality woollen spun yarns for export around the world.

Keeping left, pass through the yard of the mill whilst proceeding with care and watching out for manoeuvring vehicles. Beyond the mill, the route returns to peace and solitude and, approximately 200 metres further upstream, there is an ancient primitive weir and the entrance to what was once a covered goit. Soon after, the route once again crosses a bridge before climbing to a stone cottage where vintage cars are restored. Immediately beyond the cottage, pass through a stile on the left, and return to the valley bottom once more.

At the bottom of the descent can be found the prominent remains of Linfitts Mill. The first recorded mill was built here in the early 1750s. Powered by a 31ft waterwheel, it was used as a fulling mill and remained in occupation until the 1930s. If time allows, why not explore the ruins of this once-thriving industrial site, with many of its walls, goits and engine beds still being clearly visible in the undergrowth?

Continuing along the valley, a prominent leat can be seen on the right. Drawing water from the river, it fed the mill for operating machinery and washing textiles. A little further on, after crossing a bridge, follow a rhododendron-lined track as it makes its way up to a collection of stone dwellings at New Barn. Passing through the yard and keeping left, descend the track past Slackcote Cottages. At Slackcote Lane, turn left and, after crossing a stone bridge, follow Horest Lane as it climbs the valley's western flank. After a short climb, and adjacent to two cottages, which were part of the old Horest Mill, a signpost invites you to follow the Oldham Way Link along a private driveway towards Ashley House. A little further on, beyond the house, cross a wooden stile and continue along the Tame Valley Way. As you walk along the grassy floodplain, the tower of Christ Church, in Denshaw, can be seen rising above the tree line to the north.

At the end of the valley, a narrow footpath, which passes some animal enclosures and allotments, leads to a small exclusive housing estate, which stands on the former site of Denshaw Vale Print Works. Built in the early 1790s, the site was originally used as a woollen mill and was powered by a large waterwheel. Later it became a calico printing works. During the Second World War, the mill was used to produce camouflage netting for the Allied forces. The mill fell out of use some time in the 1950s and stood empty until it was cleared in 1996 to make way for the present housing development. Some of the original 'listed' buildings have been retained and can be seen as you walk through the estate.

Passing Printer's Cottage, continue along Buckley Drive and, where the road bends to the right, turn left and follow the narrow footpath along the side of number 16. Passing the old mill pond, go through a wrought iron gate that displays a sign saying, "walkers welcome, please close the gate" and continue along the lane to Oldham Road. After turning right, it is only a short distance to the crossroads in Denshaw.

Denshaw sits by the source of the River Tame on Saddleworth's northern fringes. Archaeological evidence indicates that the area has sustained human activity since the Stone Age and throughout the Bronze Age. The name Denshaw derives from the Old Norse language, indicating that a settlement may have existed here during the

period of the Danelaw. Consisting mainly of smallholdings, the area did not support the wool and textile industry during the Industrial Revolution, to the same extent as other nearby villages. The Junction Inn, which stands on the old Ripponden to Oldham turnpike road, was built in 1795 as a coaching house and provided rest and refreshments for travellers. In 1818, an Oddfellows Lodge was built, which still stands today in the heart of the village.

At the five-way junction, head along Huddersfield Road, where, on the left, stands Christ Church, which was built in 1863. In the church grounds, just beyond the covered gateway, stands a war memorial which bears the names of 32 local men who gave their lives in the First and Second World Wars. A little further on is the ancient hamlet of Denshaw Fold, which originally dates back to the 16th century and is the oldest surviving part of the village.

Continuing east beyond the old toll house, turn right down Wall Green where, in 1932, a Bronze Age axe, or palstave, was discovered. At Wall Green Farm, bear right and, after crossing a wooden bridge over the River Tame, bear left along a narrow fenced footpath. At the top of the short climb, make your way across the field to Ox Hey Farm, where llamas can often be seen grazing in the fields opposite. After crossing the lane, head generally south across the field to a stile on the right, just beyond the crest of the hill. After crossing the stile, follow the fence line to Lockwood Hey Farm, with its prominent arched window clearly visible in the gable end. Passing the front of the property, continue along the driveway, towards Spring Hill, and then turn left before turning right along Broad Lane towards Heights.

The picturesque 'Heights Chapel' (St Thomas Friamere) was built in 1765 and has starred in a variety of films and television programmes. Although no longer used for regular worship, it is managed by the Churches Conservation Trust. Anyone wanting to take a look inside can borrow a key from the Royal Oak Inn or the church's caretaker, whose address is listed on the door. Adjacent to the church is the Royal Oak. Known locally as, 'Heights Pub', it is reputed to serve fine ales and good wholesome meals, whilst offering a warm welcome to customers.

At the front of the pub, follow the Horseshoe Trail as the bridleway crosses several fields towards Delph Greave. Whilst descending these grassy fields, take time to admire the spectacular views of Broadstone Hill and across to the war memorial on the upper flanks of Dick Hill. Beyond lies the wild and rugged Chew Valley, with its dark gritstone edges forming the valley's jagged rim. Below and straight ahead is Delph village, with its prominent main street clearly visible, running through the centre of the village, along which you will soon be walking.

At Delph Greave, pass to the rear of the cottages and continue down the lane. Straight ahead and across the valley is Knott Hill which, coupled with a lower hill just to the south, forms what is known locally as the 'saddle' of Saddleworth. At the bottom of Lodge Lane, turn left onto Denshaw Road, before turning right at the White Lion onto High Street. A short walk along King Street, through the picturesque village of Delph, will deliver you back to the car park. With a range of hostelries and cafes situated in the village, why not enjoy a well-deserved pint in the Swan Inn or a hearty meal from Delph Fish & Chip Shop, which has to be one of the quaintest chippies in the country?

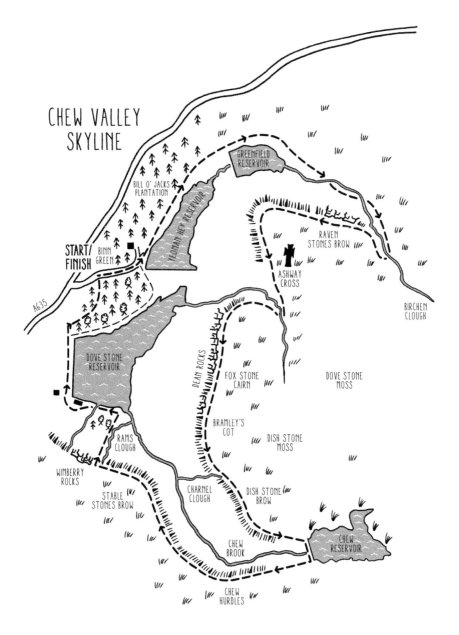

CHEW VALLEY
SKYLINE

GREENFIELD
RESERVOIR

BILL O' JACKS
PLANTATION

YEOMAN HEY RESERVOIR

RAVEN
STONES BROW

START/
FINISH

BINN
GREEN

ASHWAY
CROSS

BIRCHEN
CLOUGH

A635

DEAN ROCKS

FOX STONE
CAIRN

DOVE STONE
MOSS

DOVE STONE
RESERVOIR

BRAMLEY'S
COT

DISH STONE
MOSS

RAMS
CLOUGH

WIMBERRY
ROCKS

STABLE
STONES BROW

CHARNEL
CLOUGH

DISH STONE
BROW

CHEW
RESERVOIR

CHEW
BROOK

CHEW
HURDLES

Chew Valley Skyline

Start/Finish: *Binn Green car park. A635, Holmfirth Road*
Grid Reference: *SE 018 044*
Distance: *16 km/9.9 miles*
Ascent: *300 metres/984 feet*
Time: *5 hours*
OS Map: *Explorer OL1: The Dark Peak*

Introduction

This classic skyline route is best conducted on a clear day and offers fabulous and ever-changing views as it traverses the length of the Chew Valley edges. After a short, easy walk along the valley bottom, following Greenfield Brook, you will climb onto Raven Stones Brow and skirt along the valley edge, visiting Platt Cross, Dove Stone Rocks, Chew Reservoir and Wimberry Rocks, before descending Rams Clough to return to the valley below.

Route in brief

Binn Green – Greenfield Reservoir – Raven Stones Brow – Platt Cross – Fox Stone Cairn – Chew Reservoir – Wimberry Rocks – Dove Stone Reservoir – Binn Green

Route Description

Binn Green is located on the northern edge of Dove Stone reservoir, off the Holmfirth Road. When I was a young child, my parents used to bring me here for picnics and walks around the Chew Valley. The adjacent rocks and woods were the ideal location for a young, tireless boy to live out exciting adventures, and it is here that I made my first climbing forays on the large boulders which scatter the area.

From the information board in the lower car park, descend the steps which lead through the woods. Upon crossing a stone stile, turn left and make your way to the valley bottom via a tarmac lane, before continuing north along the shores of Yeoman Hey Reservoir. At the northern end of the reservoir, on the valley's western flanks, is the Bill o'Jacks Plantation, named after an old pub which stood close to the site.

On the evening of 2nd April 1832, the landlord, William Bradbury, and his son, Thomas, a local gamekeeper, were both violently murdered in an act that was reported at the time as "one of the most diabolical murders ever committed". An inquest, held at the King William IV public house, in Greenfield, returned a verdict of "Wilful murder by some person, or persons at present unknown".

The graves of William and Thomas Bradbury lie in the graveyard of Saddleworth (St. Chad's) Church, Uppermill. The large sandstone grave-slab, which has intrigued folk for over 180 years, bears the inscription:

Here lie the dreadfully bruised and lacerated bodies
of William Bradbury and Thomas, his son, both of
Greenfield, who were together savagely murdered in an
unusually horrid manner, on Monday night, April 2nd,
1832, William being 84 and Thomas 46 years old.

Throughout the land wherever news is read,
intelligence of their sad end has spread.
Those now who talk of far-famed Greenfield hills,
will think of Bill o' Jack's and Tom o' Bills.

Such interest did their tragic end excite.
That, here they were removed from human sight.
Thousands on thousands came to see.
The bloody scene of catastrophe.

One house, one business, and one bed.
And one most shocking death they had.
One funeral came, one inquest past.
And now one grave they had a last.

The murders were never solved and the pub became a morbid attraction for visitors, who came from far and wide to see the location of this brutal crime. The Bill o'Jacks pub, actually named the Moorcock Inn, was eventually demolished in 1937.

Continuing along the track past Greenfield Reservoir, ascend Birchen Clough to where, beyond the waterfalls, a natural ford provides passage across the stream. Following the faint grassy path, climb onto Raven Stones Brow where, adjacent to Raven Stone Rocks, stands a tower of rock known as the Trinacle.

This unique turret of gritstone rock is often frequented by local climbers. In fact, many of the crags and cliffs situated throughout the area are popular climbing venues and have been the training grounds of famous local climbers and high-altitude mountaineers such as Paul Braithwaite, who was part of the successful 1975 expedition to conquer the South-West Face of Everest and, in more recent times, professional climber and mountaineer, Kevin Thaw.

The now clear path follows the edge of Raven Stones Brow, beyond Little Flat, to Ashway Rocks. The whole route along these precipitous edges provides stunning views of the valley below. Eventually, upon nearing Ashway Rocks, the route turns south-east, following the eastern rim of Asway Gap. Along the upper path stands Platt's Cross, which is a memorial to James Platt, MP for Oldham, who was tragically killed in a shooting accident on the moors. The inscription reads: "Here by the accidental discharge of a gun, James Platt, Esq, M.P. for Oldham, lost his life - 27th August 1857".

Continuing on beyond Ashway Stone, follow the south-easterly course of the stream that flows into Asway Gap, before crossing at a natural ford. Turning north-west, the path now becomes indistinct for a short while as it crosses some boggy ground. However, before long firmer ground is once again attained as the path reaches the rocky edges of the steep valley sides.

From here on, the path follows the valley rim above Dean Rocks en route to Fox Stone Cairn, which is perched upon a large boulder. A plaque is mounted upon the rock in memory of two local climbers who lost their lives in the Italian Dolomites. The view from here across the valley is spectacular and offers a good opportunity to rest.

A little further on is a roofless ruin known as Bramley's Cot. Half built into the gritstone rocks, it is thought that it could have been an old shepherds' hut or a shooting shelter. Beyond Charnel Clough, at Dish Stone Brow, the route makes a distinct turn to the east and the path becomes less obvious as it crosses tussocky and often boggy ground en route to Chew Reservoir.

Completed in 1912, the reservoir's construction was seen as a notable feat of engineering. At 1,600 feet above sea level, it was once the highest reservoir in England. Some years ago, after a particularly harsh winter, a local fell-runner, who was competing in the Chew Valley Skyline Race, cut straight across the reservoir's frozen waters en route to the trig point on Featherbed Moss. All of the other runners, astounded by his choice of route, lagged behind the now new race leader, as they sensibly took the longer and safer route across the dam. Whilst they didn't dare follow in his footsteps, for fear of breaking through the ice, they hadn't realised that he had been carefully monitoring the thickness of the ice in the days leading up to the race.

After crossing the dam wall, turn south-west and make your way across the peaty ground towards Chew Hurdles. After a few hundred metres, firmer ground is once again reached and good progress can be made along the valley edge to Wimberry Rocks. At the locally named Indian's Head, descend the rocky gully that

is Rams Clough, allowing time to enjoy the views across the reservoir, far below. At the bottom of the descent, pass through Chew Piece Plantation and turn left along the service road towards Dove Stone Sailing Club.

From March to mid-December, the RYA affiliated club holds weekly training sessions and competitions on this 100 acre reservoir. In all weathers, scores of sailing dinghies can be seen darting back and forth as their determined crews trim their sails to ensure that their craft glide through the water with the greatest efficiency and speed.

Beyond the club house, cross the dam wall to where a set of steps provides access to a field. Turning right, follow the path along the edge of the field into some woods and, after a while, where the path forks, take the upper, left-hand option to reach a lane. Crossing the lane, climb the stone stile and make the final short ascent to return to the car park at Binn Green.

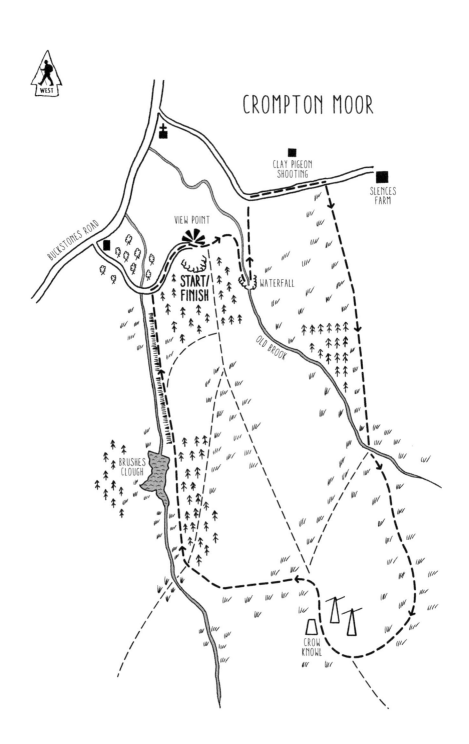

CROMPTON MOOR

WEST

CLAY PIGEON
SHOOTING

SLENCES
FARM

BUCKSTONES ROAD

VIEW POINT

START/
FINISH

WATERFALL

OLD BROOK

BRUSHES
CLOUGH

CROW
KNOWL

Crompton Moor:
A walk of ever unfolding views

Start: *Brushes Clough Car Park*
Grid Reference: *SD 951 100*
Distance: *4.3 km/2.6 miles*
Ascent: *320 metres/1,017 feet*
Time: *2 hours*
OS Map: *Explorer 277: Manchester & Salford*

Introduction

This short walk circumnavigates Crompton Moor and offers constantly changing views throughout its course. When I was a child, my father would bring me for walks here, as did my grandfather with his young son before that, and these early forays upon the moor instilled into me an undying love for the hills and moors of Saddleworth. This small oasis of moorland is criss-crossed by a myriad of paths and bridleways which, when the walk is complete, leave plenty of opportunity for further exploration of the area's diverse landscape and historic sites.

Route in Brief

Brushes Clough – Pingot Quarry – Crow Knowl – Brushes Clough Reservoir – Brushes Clough

Route Description

Lying to the west of Denshaw, Crompton Moor, anciently known as High Moor, is a gateway to the South Pennines. Managed by Oldham Countryside Service, the 160 acres of moorland and woods were designated as a Site of Biological Importance (SBI) in 2003. The diverse mixture of purple moor-grass, heather, wet bog and woodland supports a wealth of wildlife. Following the Enclosure Acts of the 18th century, several small farms were built upon the moor and the remains of some of them can still be seen today. Several coal mines were also excavated and the disused pits and spoil heaps remain as evidence from times gone by. In the late 19th century, sandstone quarrying took place here, too, in the largest of which the car park is now located. In times past, the remoteness and inaccessibility of the area proved to be an ideal location for local men to gather and hold 'tossing schools', illegal gambling sessions that were often held here in a bid to evade the law.

Before embarking on the walk, take a few moments to stand at the view point overlooking the town of Shaw. The information plaque built into the stone wall indicates a range of places which can be viewed from this elevated spot. On a clear day, Winter Hill, with its 1,015 ft transmitting mast, can be seen straight ahead, to the west. To the left sits Fiddlers Ferry power station, outside Warrington. On 13th January 1984, one of the coal-fired power station's massive cooling towers collapsed due to freak high winds.

Turning to the right of the view point, pass through a stile in the stone wall adjacent to an information board, and descend the managed path to the left, signposted 'Oldham Way'. From here, Scout Moor Wind Farm can be seen high above Rochdale. With its 26 Nordex N80 wind turbines, it is the largest onshore wind farm in England.

At the bottom of the path is one of Oldham's hidden secrets. Crompton Waterfall cascades over the edge of Pingot Quarry and in wet weather is truly an impressive sight. Fed by Old Brook, water drains off the moor and follows its downstream course to the River Beal.

After admiring this little-known eighth natural wonder of the world, continue along the path, cross a wooden horse-stile and follow the tarmac lane to the right, towards Slences Farm. Approximately 200 metres further on is a clay pigeon shooting range on the left. Whilst passage along the lane is within the safe area, if shooting is in progress, it is advised to make your presence known to the lookouts before continuing.

At the gate to Slences Farm, marked "PRIVATE", turn right and follow the obvious path uphill which handrails the stone wall. Whilst ascending the path, a backward glance will reveal far-reaching views over Manchester. Nearing the top of the climb, the communications masts on Crow Knowl come into view and a glance to the right will provide a glimpse of the car park at Brushes Clough where the walk began. Continue upwards through a horse-stile marked "permissive path" and, when the climb is complete the Millennium Cross will come into view, standing proud on Besom Hill. Slightly to the left is the Bishops Park monument.

Following the path downhill, pass through a metal gate and, crossing the upper reaches of Old Brook, continue along the track as it sweeps to the left and rises over Little Rochdale Parish. At the top of the rise, the communications mast on Windy Hill can be seen standing tall against the skyline, and the rocky ridge that is Blackstone Edge lies to the north. In the foreground lies Rooden Reservoir, one of five reservoirs situated in the Peithorne Valley. Each of these locations is visited when undertaking other walks detailed within this book.

At this point, the path meets a more prominent vehicle track which should be followed to the south-east. Along this track, Millstone Edge comes into sight, with the prominent wedge-shaped summit of West Nab visible beyond. Slightly to the right sits the Holme Moss transmitting station, towering above Black Hill's dark peaty plateau.

Continue onwards for the short distance to the summit trig point which stands within the site of Crow Knowl telecommunications station. If the air is still and the day warm, why not sit for a while and run your eyes once more over the many views already seen so far, for this hill offers a fine vista throughout the full range of the compass. One sight which remains yet to be enjoyed is the gritstone edges of the Chew Valley, which tower above the Dove Stone Reservoir, approximately 7 miles to the south-east.

Heading south-west, leave the summit and descend the track. With the masts now to your back, Oldham's Civic Centre building can be seen standing tall over the ridgeline of Oldham Edge. Upon reaching an obvious stony track, descend the footpath which forks left, from where Bishops Park monument can once again be seen straight ahead. Standing at 1,233 feet above sea level, it is the highest point in Oldham. After only a few metres, cross a wooden stile and continue downhill following the path marked Oldham Way and Crompton Circuit. Ignoring all other paths keep going until Brushes Clough Reservoir comes into view.

On a nice summer's, day this small pocket of water is a pleasant spot to linger and watch the ducks and other water birds which frequent these still waters. When

my son was younger, he always enjoyed walking over these moors and we would often stop here awhile so that he could skim stones and explore the nearby woods.

Keeping to the main track, which now levels off and traverses above the reservoir and its outflow, continue west where Tandle Hill Country Park soon emerges on the skyline ahead. This 110 acre site of mixed woodland is Oldham's oldest country park. Now designated as a Site of Biological Importance, due to its fungi and bird populations, it was once used by political demonstrators for practising marching and drilling formations in the period leading up to the Peterloo massacre, which took place in Manchester on 16th August 1819. After that fateful day, beech trees were planted to prevent any further marching practice, and the area became a private hunting park and game reserve. In 1919, the park was gifted to the people of Royton by Councillor Norris Bradbury, as a peace offering to mark the end of the First World War.

Ignoring a small path on the right, keep to the main track which handrails a stone wall on the left. The old quarry workings to the right have now been turned into a mountain biking area, so keep an eye out for bikers who may be riding along this section of bridleway. Only a short walk further on, and the track emerges onto the road. Turning right into the quarry car park will bring to an end this walk of ever unfolding views.

NORTH

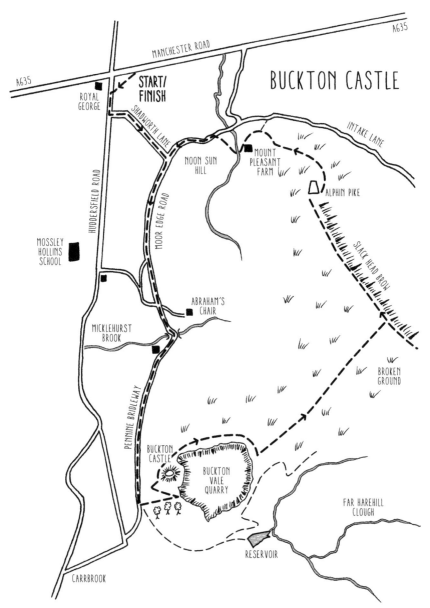

A635

MANCHESTER ROAD

A635

BUCKTON CASTLE

ROYAL GEORGE

START/ FINISH

SHADWORTH LANE

INTAKE LANE

HUDDERSFIELD ROAD

NOON SUN HILL

MOUNT PLEASANT FARM

ALPHIN PIKE

MOOR EDGE ROAD

MOSSLEY HOLLINS SCHOOL

SLACK HEAD BROW

ABRAHAM'S CHAIR

MICKLEHURST BROOK

BROKEN GROUND

PENNINE BRIDLEWAY

BUCKTON CASTLE

BUCKTON VALE QUARRY

FAR HAREHILL CLOUGH

RESERVOIR

CARRBROOK

Buckton Castle

Start: *Royal George. A635, Mossley Road.*

Grid Reference: *SD 985 036*

Distance: *8.2 km/5 miles*

Ascent: *430 metres/1,378 feet*

Time: *3.5 hours*

OS Map: *Explorer OL1: The Dark Peak*

Introduction

This short moorland walk makes an initial, heart-pumping climb up Shadworth Lane before following the course of the Pennine Bridleway along Moor Edge Road. Overlooking Carrbrook, a short but steep climb through the heather will deliver you to the ancient remains of Buckton Castle, from where you will enjoy commanding views of the surrounding landscape.

Skirting around the rim of Buckton Vale Quarry, you will climb the southern, heather-clad slopes of Alphin Pike to the summit shelter adjacent to the trig point. From this lofty position you can, once again, relish far-reaching vistas.

After enjoying the views, an obvious path will take you on a steep descent down Alphin Brow to the ruins of Mount Pleasant Farm, from where the Oldham Way is followed below Noonsun Hill and back down Shadworth Lane, to return to the Royal George.

Route in brief

Royal George – Moor Edge Road – Buckton Castle – Alphin Pike – Shadworth Lane – Royal George

Route Description

From the lay-by to the east of the Royal George, take the short section of footpath which provides safe passage to Huddersfield Road. Turning left towards Mossley Hollins, cross the carriageway, for there is no footpath on the nearside. After approximately 100 metres, turn left onto Shadworth Lane, where an old boundary stone can just be seen, concealed in the verge. At the top of the climb, turn right and follow the Tameside Trail along Moor Edge Lane, from where you will enjoy clear views over Mossley, with Hartshead Pike standing prominently on the skyline. Beyond Top o'th' Green Cottage, and after passing under some pylons, fork right down the track before crossing Micklehurst Brook. As you regain higher ground, Micklehurst Cricket Club comes into view. Formed in 1890 by employees of George Lawton and Sons, a local woollen manufacturer, the club has enjoyed many local successes.

Further on, the track drops away steeply and Carrbrook comes into view, beyond which the heather-clad slopes of Harridge Pike dominate the skyline. A few metres further on, before reaching a quarry access road, turn left and leave the Pennine Bridleway to enter access land along a beaten track, which soon widens out into a grassy path, the entrance to which has been blocked off with large boulders to prevent vehicular access. Skirting along the upper reaches of an oak plantation, a fence is reached which forms the boundary of Buckton Vale Quarry. Clear signage warns people to "KEEP OUT". Approaching the fence, turn sharp left along a narrow path which makes a short but steep climb through the heather to reach the ancient site of Buckton Castle.

Whilst some historians originally thought that the castle could have previously been the site of an Iron Age hill fort, many now believe, after archaeological excavations were conducted, that the remains of the stone castle are actually from around the 12th

century, when it was built by William de Neville, Lord of Longdendale. No matter who first chose this lofty position, when standing upon the fort's foundations, you can appreciate the commanding view that would have been afforded from atop the castle's ramparts. The views are far reaching and any stealthy approach would have been a difficult task.

From the castle, follow the northern edge of the quarry, which is a horrible scar on what is otherwise an unspoilt landscape. At grid: 996 019 follow a faint trod through the heather to pick up a 4 x 4 track which is not marked on the map. Ignoring the other prominent track, which is located a little over to the east and marked on the OS 1:25,000 map of the area, follow the wheel tracks, which meander generally north-east across the open moor. Nearing the top of the climb, the track peters out to nothing more than a narrow path and makes its way onto Slack Head Brow. Reaching the watershed, turn north-west along a clear path which leads directly to the summit shelter and trig point on Alphin Pike. From this towering position, superb views are to be enjoyed which, on a clear day, extend as far as the Snowdonia mountains.

From the summit, follow the heavily eroded path through the heather which descends the hill and offers clear views of some of Saddleworth's villages. At Greave, the path improves and handrails a fence line to emerge onto a stony lane. Crossing the stile, adjacent to a gate, pass the ruins of Mount Pleasant Farm, which a former tenant once described as, "Pleasant in summer, misery in winter". Beyond the ruins, continue along the Oldham Way around the foot of Noonsun Hill, where you can often see pheasant strutting amongst the heather. Emerging onto Lane Head, adjacent to Hill Cottage, turn left along the lane. Beyond Noonsun Farm, built in 1795, turn right and descend Shadworth Lane again, to return to the Royal George.

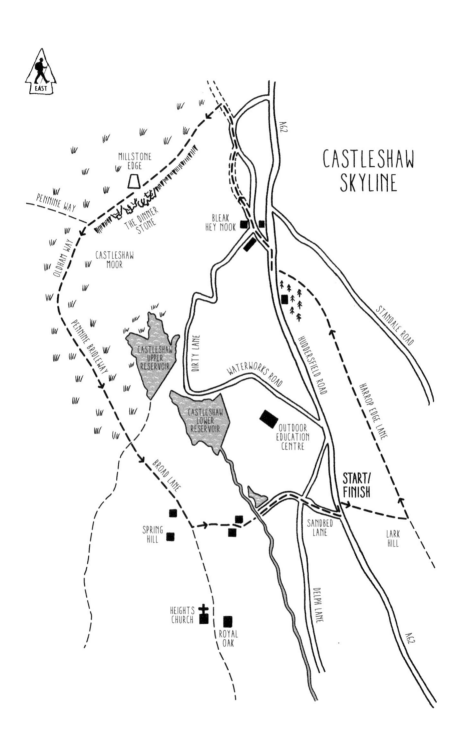

EAST

CASTLESHAW
SKYLINE

MILLSTONE
EDGE

PENNINE WAY

THE DINNER STONE

OLDHAM WAY

CASTLESHAW
MOOR

PENNINE BRIDLEWAY

CASTLESHAW
UPPER
RESERVOIR

DIRTY LANE

CASTLESHAW
LOWER
RESERVOIR

BROAD LANE

SPRING
HILL

HEIGHTS
CHURCH

ROYAL
OAK

A62

BLEAK
HEY NOOK

WATERWORKS ROAD

HUDDERSFIELD ROAD

STANDALE ROAD

HARROP EDGE LANE

OUTDOOR
EDUCATION
CENTRE

START/
FINISH

SANDBED
LANE

LARK
HILL

DELPH LANE

A62

Castleshaw Skyline

Start: *Layby on east-bound side of A62, Huddersfield Road.*
Grid Reference: *SD 992 081*
Distance: *11.5 km/7.1 miles*
Ascent: *400 metres/1,312 feet*
Time: *4 hours*
OS Maps: *Explorer OL1: The Dark Peak and OL21: South Pennines*

Introduction

This is a classic horseshoe, ridgeline walk with very little climbing involved. On a clear day, the route offers stunning views, with many of Saddleworth's prominent landmarks being in view. Maintaining high ground throughout most of its course, the route circumnavigates the picturesque Castleshaw Valley in which sits the foundations of a Roman fort, which once guarded, what was at the time the northernmost reaches of the Roman Empire.

Route in brief

Huddersfield Road – Lark Hill – Standedge – Castleshaw Moor – Broad Lane – Heights – Huddersfield Road.

Route Description

From the lay-by adjacent to the junction of Sand Bed Lane, cross Huddersfield Road to where a wooden stile provides passage into a field. From this point, the route starts with a short, but awakening, climb along a path which ascends in a south-westerly direction across two fields. At the top of the climb, pass through a stile and turn left onto Harrop Edge Lane. From this vantage point, the whole picturesque route can be admired, encouraging oxygen-starved legs to stride out.

Heading north-west, follow this unsurfaced lane, which runs the full length of Lark Hill. This long whaleback hill separates two valleys, in which nestle the villages of Delph and Diggle. Taking great care, cross the busy A62 and turn right before turning left onto Standedge Foot Road. Follow the lane for approximately 300m and, immediately after Bleak Hey Nook Lane, pass through a gate adjacent to a farm building. This grassy track, called Whimberry Lee Lane, is a section of the old turnpike road which ascends for approximately 600m before passing through two gates where horses are often grazed and signs politely remind walkers to close the gates.

Re-emerging onto Standedge Foot Lane, pass the entrance to Rock Farm B&B and, ignoring the sharp right-hand bend, continue straight ahead along the rough track. This section of the Pennine Bridleway is popular with mountain bikers, as it shares its course with a local mountain biking route known as 'The Diggle Jiggle'. Upon reaching the top of the climb, a signpost directs the way north along the Pennine Way, which was the first long-distance footpath to be established in the UK.

Passing through a kissing gate, proceed north for the short climb to the trig point on Standedge. This rocky ridgeline, also known as Millstone Edge, provides a commanding vantage point from which to admire the Castleshaw Valley below. This exposed gritstone edge is notorious for its cold winds and is no place to linger in bad weather. However, if the weather is good, a search of the rocks below the trig point will reveal several plaques in memory of various individuals. One such plaque,

located near the Dinner Stone, marks the spot from which the ashes of the famous Saddleworth writer and poet, Ammon Wrigley, were scattered. A statue of Ammon Wrigley can also be seen in Uppermill.

From the trig point, continue along the Pennine Way until a stone marker post is reached at a path junction, nestled in a small gully. This post directs Pennine Way walkers to turn right and leave Standedge completely in order to continue their northbound pilgrimage. However, the skyline route continues north-west along the course of the Oldham Way, which now leaves the rocky edge and breaks out across Castleshaw Moor until a large cairn is reached on Hind Hill. Whilst marked with a series of small cairns, and wooden posts, the path is less obvious, and care should be taken in poor visibility.

From the cairn, enjoy the grassy descent as the path heads south-west until a gate is reached in a stone wall. Passing through the gate, follow an old walled track,

called Moor Lane, to the junction at Four Lane Ends. On the left, just before the gate, is a set of stone steps used by horse riders for mounting and dismounting their steeds. On the back face of these steps is carved the inscription, "PBW – The Edith Boon Way". Edith Boon was one of three founding members of the Saddleworth Pony Club, back in the 1960s. A book The journeys of Edith Boon MBE, was written about her by fellow founder Barbara Haigh.

Maintaining the high ground, continue straight ahead along another narrow lane, which can be rather muddy during wet conditions, and climb towards an area known as 'Heights'. At the top of the climb, on Broad Lane, stands a house on the right, outside which a stone bench is positioned at the end of the drive. On the front of the bench is written, "In loving memory: To Mum, Barbara Burton, 1934 – 1999. These are the hills that she walked and the garden that she created. So take a seat and rest your tired feet, have a rest and view the best. From her daughters Lynne and Deborah".

After taking a seat and enjoying the views, continue the short distance to where, opposite the entrance to another large property called Spring Hill, a signpost marked

Horseshoe Trail indicates the way down a narrow, sunken packhorse trail called Hey Flake Lane. At the bottom of the descent, turn left and then immediately right, past two cottages named Charity Farm and Clough Farm, which were built in the 1700s. From here, the bridleway continues its steep shaded descent and care should be taken, as the old, worn paving slabs can be very slippery underfoot.

This area, which is known as Grange, was part of Friarmere, which in turn was part of the Roche Abbey estate. Local historians believe that the Black Friars had a house or 'Grange' near here which possibly lends its name to the area.

The route eventually emerges into sunlight and a ford is reached, which in hot weather offers a welcoming reprieve for hot, tired feet. For those not wanting to get their feet wet, a small wooden footbridge can be crossed a little further upstream. Once across the stream, the route continues along Hull Mill Lane and past the old mill lodge which served Hull Mill. Built in the 1700s by John Scholefield, it eventually fell into disuse in the 1980s and was demolished to make way for a new housing development. At the crossroads, continue straight ahead along Sandbed Lane to return to the lay-by on Huddersfield Road.

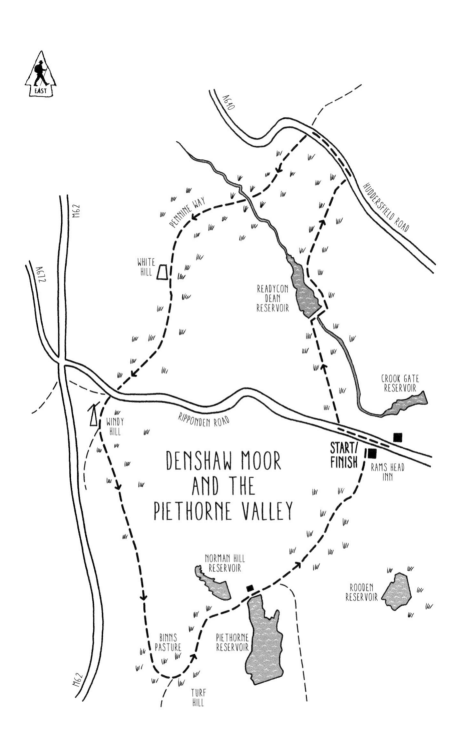

EAST

A640

PENNINE WAY

M62

A672

WHITE HILL

READYCON DEAN RESERVOIR

HUDDERSFIELD ROAD

CROOK GATE RESERVOIR

WINDY HILL

RIPPONDEN ROAD

START/ FINISH

RAMS HEAD INN

DENSHAW MOOR
AND THE
PIETHORNE VALLEY

NORMAN HILL RESERVOIR

ROODEN RESERVOIR

M62

BINNS PASTURE

PIETHORNE RESERVOIR

TURF HILL

Denshaw Moor and the Piethorne Valley

Start: *Rams Head Inn. A672, Ripponden Road*
Grid Reference: *SD 977 119*
Distance: *11.6 km/7.2 miles*
Ascent: *590 metres/1,935 feet*
Time: *4 hours*
OS Maps: *Explorer OL21: South Pennines*

Introduction

Following mainly obvious tracks, footpaths and bridleways, this spectacular walk makes an initial crossing of Denshaw Moor before heading north along the Pennine Way National Trail and traversing the windswept landscape of the Marsden Moor Estate. From Windy Hill, you will descend into the Piethorne Valley, with its five major reservoirs, before making a final, lung-busting, climb to return to the Rams Head Inn.

Route in Brief

Rams Head Inn - Readycon Dean Reservoir – White Hill – Rook Stones Hill – Tunshill Lane - Piethorne Reservoir – Rams Head Inn

Route Description

Starting from the lay-by on the A672 opposite the 450 year old Rams Head Inn, head generally north along the offside of Ripponden Road. After only a few metres, a narrow section of bridleway provides safe passage from the traffic, until a gate is reached beyond a small compound. Turning right, proceed along a wide track which leads to the secluded and seldom visited Readycon Dean Reservoir.

Nestled in a quiet little valley, Radycon Dean Reservoir sits at the source of the River Tame. Its moorland waters eventually converge with the River Goyt before flowing into the River Mersey and then out into the saline waters of Liverpool Bay.

Crossing the dam, continue along the southern edge of the reservoir before climbing over Denshaw Moor to meet the A640 Denshaw to Huddersfield Road. At the end of the track, turn left and, taking care, for there is no footpath, ascend the road for approximately 500m before turning left onto the Pennine Way. From here, the Pennine Way is followed across the Marsden Moor Estate, which is now managed by the National Trust, after it was conveyed to them by the Radcliffe family in 1955 in lieu of death duties. Upon reaching the trig point on White Hill, make your descent to the A672 at Windy Hill.

Crossing to the large unsurfaced lay-by, continue north along the Pennine Way for a short distance, until a service road is reached which leads to the communications mast on Rook Stones Hill, also known as Windy Hill. At the end of the road, follow a track to the northern corner of the compound before heading

west and dropping down to an undulating ridgeline known as Windy Hills. From this vantage point, the M62 motorway can be seen below, with thousands of vehicles flowing in an ant-like procession along this busy trans-Pennine highway.

Following the course of a broken wall, an often muddy bridleway eventually descends along a sunken lane before terminating at the junction with Tunshill Lane. Turning left, follow the Rochdale Way, which steadily climbs between Turf Hill and Binns Pasture before making its descent to the valley floor. At the bottom of the descent, pass through a gate adjacent to a small wood, and pass a stone building which stands at the head of Piethorne Reservoir. Built in 1866, this is the largest reservoir in the valley. In the mid-18th century, a 5 inch Celtic Spear head was found here, leading historians to believe that the valley and surrounding area could have sustained human habitation since the Iron Age.

Leaving the reservoir behind, climb the steep track, which is a former packhorse route, for the final lung-busting ascent back to the Rams Head Inn. If you have planned your return to coincide with opening hours, a well-earned pint can now be relished.

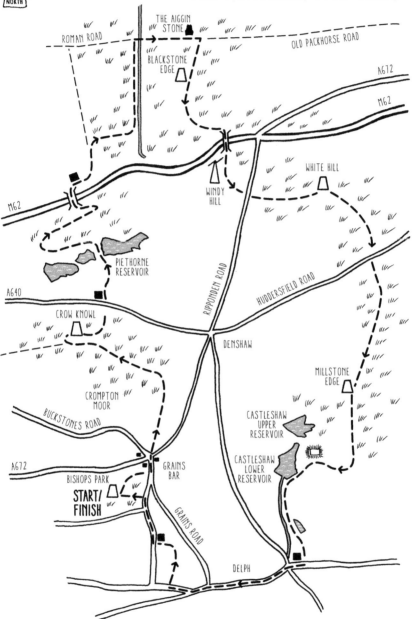

THE NORTHERN FIVE TRIGS

NORTH

ROMAN ROAD

THE AIGGIN STONE

OLD PACKHORSE ROAD

BLACKSTONE EDGE

A672

M62

M62

WINDY HILL

WHITE HILL

M62

PIETHORNE RESERVOIR

A640

RIPPONDEN ROAD

HUDDERSFIELD ROAD

CROW KNOWL

DENSHAW

MILLSTONE EDGE

CROMPTON MOOR

CASTLESHAW UPPER RESERVOIR

BUCKSTONES ROAD

CASTLESHAW LOWER RESERVOIR

A672

GRAINS BAR

BISHOPS PARK

START/ FINISH

GRAINS ROAD

DELPH

The Northern Five Trigs

Start/Finish: *Bishops Park car park*
Grid Reference: *SD 966 083*
Distance: *32.1km/19.9 miles*
Ascent: *1,210 metres/3,969 feet*
Time: *8 hours*
OS Map: *Explorer OL1: The Dark Peak and OL21: South Pennines*

Introduction

The sister route to the Saddleworth Five Trigs, this slightly easier walk follows mainly prominent footpaths throughout its course. Starting on the northern fringes of Saddleworth, the route crosses the Piethorne Valley and Clegg Moor before climbing a well-preserved section of Roman road onto Blackstone Edge. Turning south, you will follow the Pennine Way over White Hill to Millstone Edge before descending into the Castleshaw Valley and past the site of an ancient Roman fort. Upon reaching the picturesque village of Delph, a short, easy walk along Hill Top Lane will deliver you to the final trig point at Bishops Park.

Route in brief

Bishops Park – Crow Knowl – Blackstone Edge – White Hill – Millstone Edge – Bishops Park

Route Description

This northern five trig points walk, often referred to as the 'New Five Trigs', starts from Bishops Park at the source of the River Medlock. Bishops Park was named after William and Anne Bishop and donated "for the use and benefit of the people of Oldham and district".

From the car park, below the monument, turn left along Ship Lane and then left again onto Grains Road. At the crossroads, at Grains Bar, stands an old toll house. The term 'bar' derives from the bar which was placed across the road to prevent further passage until the correct fee was paid.

A faint footpath at the top of Buckstones Road leads past the rear of a bungalow, called Pottery Hill Farm, situated on the left hand side of the A672. Initially, the route follows the course of the Crompton Circuit along a walled path before breaking tracks, via a stone stile, into a field on the right. Following the course of the wall, continue through the fields before climbing a stile adjacent to a gate. Turning right, cross another stile to reach an often muddy lane. Continuing straight ahead, past a house on the right, gradually ascend an old lane to a small wooden gate. After

passing through the gate, handrail the stone wall on the right for the short climb up Tame Scout that will deliver you onto the open moor. It is believed that the word 'scout' derives from the ancient word 'scwd', which means steep. On a clear day, New Years Bridge Reservoir, with its prominent overflow, can be seen at the head of the Tame Valley, above the village of Denshaw.

Continuing straight ahead, follow the faint footpath past a small pond to a wall corner, before bearing left along a faint trod. Upon reaching a prominent track, a slightly narrower, but equally obvious, track crosses Crompton Moor, following the line of pylons, towards the masts upon Crow Knowl. Leaving the open moor via a wooden stile, a prominent vehicle track is reached which runs below Crow Knowl. Turning left, follow the Crompton Circuit along this track for approximately 100 metres before turning right at a junction and following the obvious route to the summit and the first trig point of the day.

From Crow Knowl, take the track, which is the Oldham Way, down to the A640. Crossing the road with care, continue straight ahead along the track to the right of the house which used to be the Moorcock Inn. At the top of the lane, turn left where a stile on the right provides access into a field. Following the legal right of way, cross two enclosed fields before handrailing the course of a stone wall across several broken fields until a stile is reached on the left. After crossing the stile, follow the path downhill until it emerges onto the reservoir road. There are five major reservoirs situated in the Piethorne Valley, all of which are under the control of United Utilities.

Crossing the dam wall of the Piethorne Reservoir, turn left to follow the track for just over a mile around the bottom of Town Hill, to a crossroads at Tunshill Lane. Continuing north, follow the Pennine Bridleway as it descends into the valley below, where the track turns east and follows the upstream course of Longden End Brook. After a short while, a small bridge provides passage over the stream and the route climbs uphill, keeping to the west of a disused farm

building at New Nook. At the top of the climb, a track crosses a bridge over the M62 motorway before turning right to a small farm cottage. Crossing the yard, pass through a gate and, after crossing the field, continue northwards along the bridleway. After a short while, a hidden path leads through the bracken and follows the course of the pylons before climbing Clegg Moor and onto Hoar Edge. Soon the footpath leads to Broad Head Drain, which provides a constant supply of water to Blackstone Edge Reservoir. After following the drain for about a mile, turn right and climb the Roman road to the Aiggin Stone.

This section of the Roman road, which crosses Blackstone Edge, is very well preserved, with the paving slabs and central drainage channel being clear underfoot. At the top of the climb, adjacent to the ancient way-marker called the Aiggin Stone, the route now turns south over a wooden stile and follows a rocky path along the Pennine Way. When visibility is poor, the route is less obvious and a few small cairns and wooden marker posts guide the way to the second triangulation pillar, which stands at the summit of Blackstone Edge.

If the weather is fair, this is a lovely spot to rest a while and enjoy the far-reaching views which unfold to the west, overlooking Littleborough and Rochdale. The distinctive wedge shape of Winter Hill, with its 1,015ft transmission tower, can be seen in the distance. To the south-west, the view stretches out across Oldham and Manchester and over the Cheshire plain to the mountains of Snowdonia beyond.

From here on, continue southward to cross Longden End Brook, just below its source, before making the short climb which leads to the footbridge that crosses the busy M62 motorway. After crossing the bridge, the path ascends to a large unsurfaced lay-by on the A672, at Windy Hill. From here, taking care crossing the road, go through a wooden gate and ascend the maintained path to the trig point on White Hill.

After touching the third trig point of the day, descend the path and cross a small stream which is the source of the River Tame. Making the short climb to the flat summit of Rape Hill, descend the other side to the A640 Denshaw

to Huddersfield Road. From Haigh Gutter, continue south along the Pennine Way to the fourth trig point upon the rocky edge that is Standedge. Known locally as Millstone Edge, the gritstone rocks were quarried here to produce mill stones, which were used in grist mills to grind grain into flour.

With only one trig point remaining, continue south and, after leaving the open moor, cross some walled fields to where a wooden kissing gate delivers you onto a rough track. Turning right, descend the Standedge Trail and continue along the lane to Bleak Hey Nook. At the rear of the now derelict Horse & Jockey pub, a fingerpost directs you right onto Bleak Hey Nook Lane for the ½ mile walk to Castle Shaw. Just beyond Castleshaw House, at a sharp right-hand bend, a wooden stile provides access to the ancient remains of Castleshaw Roman Fort.

Constructed around AD79, the fort protected what was then the northern limits of the Roman Empire. Designated as a Scheduled Ancient Monument, the original stronghold covered over three acres and garrisoned around 500 infantry soldiers. After some fifteen years of occupation, it was abandoned when the army pushed further north and therefore reorganised its strategic defences. The fort was reoccupied in the early 2nd century A.D. as a small outpost, and was one of a series of Roman fortifications intended to protect the military road between Chester and York.

From the south-west corner of the fort, follow the sign directing the way to the car park and descend the field to Cote Lane. After turning right, bear left along the dam wall of Castleshaw Lower Reservoir. A sign reads, "private road – footpath only". At the southernmost point of the dam, where it makes a definite turn, descend the embankment via a set of steps and follow the footpath along the valley bottom. Following the course of Hull Brook, the route passes Hull Mill Lodge and Eagle Mill Dam before emerging onto Delph Lane adjacent to the White Lion public house. Turning right, make your way through the picturesque village of Delph where several hostelries provide suitable refreshments.

With the walk nearing its end, ascend Stoneswood Road to the right of the Millgate Arts Centre & Library, and then turn immediate right onto Woodhouse Knowl. Beyond the cottages, the lane becomes a grassy track and then a narrow footpath, as it skirts past the rear of several houses on Grains Road. After crossing a stile, the path ascends open ground before turning left along a stone wall. Soon, another stile is crossed and the route passes through the front garden of Hill Top Cottages, once the home of Saddleworth writer and poet, Ammon Wrigley. Emerging onto Hill Top Lane, turn right and follow its course along Badger Edge to where, beyond High Lee Lane, a bridleway leads to the Bishops Park monument and the final trig point of the day. From this vantage point, and if the skies are clear, much of the route can be observed, allowing you to reflect on the day's walk.

EAST

DIGLEY RESERVOIR

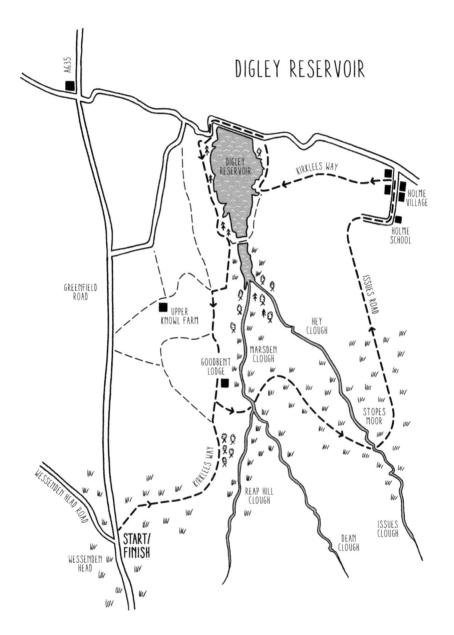

A635

DIGLEY RESERVOIR

KIRKLEES WAY

HOLME VILLAGE

HOLME SCHOOL

ISSUES ROAD

GREENFIELD ROAD

UPPER KNOWL FARM

HEY CLOUGH

MARSDEN CLOUGH

GOODBENT LODGE

STOPES MOOR

KIRKLEES WAY

WESSENDEN HEAD ROAD

REAP HILL CLOUGH

ISSUES CLOUGH

DEAN CLOUGH

START/ FINISH

WESSENDEN HEAD

Digley Reservoir

Start: *Wessenden Head. A635 Saddleworth/Holmfirth Road.*
Grid Reference: *SE 077 072*
Distance: *11.8 km/7.3 miles*
Ascent: *340 metres/1,049 feet*
Time: *4 hours*
Map: *Explorer OL1: The Dark Peak*

Introduction

Although outside Saddleworth proper, this walk is definitely worth the drive over Saddleworth Moor, into West Yorkshire. A local beauty spot popular with walkers, Digley Reservoir lies just north of the little village of Holme and sits below the north-east flank of Black Hill, which towers dominantly above. This is an easy to follow, low-level route that visits some interesting and picturesque locations and is an ideal bad weather alternative to venturing high onto Black Hill and the surrounding moorlands.

Route in brief

Wessenden Head – Black Pool Bridge – Good Bent – Stopes Moor – Issues Road – Holme – Digley Wood – Digley Quarry – Good Bent Lodge – Wessenden Head

Route Description

From Wessenden Head, opposite the junction with Wessenden Head Road, follow the Kirklees Way as it descends to some woods above Reap Hill Clough. From here, the route follows a rough and often muddy lane, bordered with broken walls on either side, and eventually merges with the junction of Nether Lane and Springs Road. Bearing right, follow Nether Lane for approximately 100 metres before crossing a stone stile. Heading south, descend the field towards Black Pool Bridge. At the bottom of the field, cross a rickety wooden stile and continue along the clear path as it descends into the delightful Marsden Clough.

Black Pool Bridge, so called because of a deep dark pool nearby, crosses the river at the convergence of Reap Hill Clough and Dean Clough where the dark peaty waters from Wessenden Head Moor flow into Bilberry Reservoir, just over 1 kilometre further downstream.

In the early hours of 5th February 1852, after a sustained period of heavy rain, the Bilberry Reservoir dam burst, sending over 86 million gallons of water in a raging torrent down the River Holme. Eighty-one people, most of whom were asleep in their beds, lost their lives on that fateful night.

After crossing the bridge and leaving behind this small but delightfully wild and remote-looking valley, continue along the path as it climbs up onto the heather clad moor and crosses Good Bent. At the top of the climb, the path sweeps round to the south-west and passes several shooting butts, which are an obvious indication that this is prime grouse shooting land. At a ford, cross the stream which runs out of Issues Clough and follow the path as it sweeps round to the east across Stopes Moor, towards a series of walled fields.

Upon reaching the dry-stone walls, which are the only barrier preventing the moor from reclaiming these pasture fields, cross through an old wrought iron kissing gate onto the long straight walled track called Issues Road. Continue along this old lane for approximately 1,200 metres to where, from the high ground, Digley Reservoir can be seen, sitting at the head of the Holme Valley. A few metres further on, the track bends round to the right and becomes a tarmacked lane called Meal Hill Road, which heads south past a small school on its descent into the village of Holme, which was laid waste by William the Conqueror for rebelling against Norman rule.

Holme School, with its distinctive bell tower, was a Board School until 1891, when free education was provided as a result of the Elementary Education Act. According to a document entitled: Township of Holme – Earnshaw's Charity, a school house was first built on the site with money bequeathed by Joshua Earnshaw, who died in 1798. According to the records, it was rebuilt in 1820, after becoming dilapidated and a schoolmaster's house was added in 1838.

Approximately 150 metres past the school, a way marker indicates a left turn along a narrow walled footpath, where once again the Kirklees Way is followed. After passing through a stone squeeze stile and heading in a northerly direction, follow the footpath across several fields, to where Digley Reservoir can yet again be seen.

Upon leaving the fields, the grassy footpath descends for a short while to meet a managed path running in from Bilberry Reservoir to the west. At this location stands a wooden bench in memory of a 15 year old boy who sadly died of a brain aneurysm whilst playing football. A plaque mounted upon the bench reads, "Huw Thatcher, 1995 – 2011 'Remembering Huw for his free spirit and happy times here at Digley'. So much love, Mum, Dad & Cas xxx". In memory of Huw, his family set up the Huw Thatcher Trust to raise funds for the Brain Injury Rehabilitation Trust (BIRT), which helps people to recover from various types of brain injury.

Now turn south-east along the clear path which parallels Digley Wood, on the southern shores of the reservoir, to Digley South car park. Crossing the car park, turn left along the road and cross the dam wall. At the northern end of the dam, follow the road round to the left and, after approximately 100 metres, pass through a wooden gate marked, "footpath to the picnic site avoiding the road" and follow the path leading to the car park at Digley Quarry.

From the car park, a footpath heads west following the course of an old narrow, walled cart track past Alison quarry and through a small mixed wood. Arriving at a path junction, take the left-hand fork, following the course of the Kirklees Way, where the path descends for a short while through a small mixed wood, before dropping onto the shores of Digley Reservoir. Here, the cart track is lost to the dark waters of the reservoir but, continuing westward across the shoreline and, crossing a stream, the route heads for a large stone gatepost at the end of a broken wall, where the way becomes clear underfoot, once again, as the track emerges from the water.

Alternative route: If the water level is high in the reservoir, this section of route may be impassable, in which case the following alternative can be taken. At the path junction (Grid: 107 072), take the path which forks off to the right on higher ground. Keeping the woods to the left and the fields to the right, drop down a set of concrete steps before turning right at the end of the fence to rejoin the walled lane which comes in from the left (Grid: 106 072).

On the left-hand side of the lane, just beyond a definite left-hand bend, two large stone gateposts mark the site of an old property. Lying within the grounds, and amongst the piles of rubble, the remains of the old castellated walls can still be seen.

A few metres further on and the view opens up, offering an impressive vista, with Hey Clough and Marsden Clough nestled either side of the heathery spur which is Good Bent End. At a forked junction, take the right-hand track and continue uphill along the Kirklees Way towards Greaves Head. At a T-junction, turn left onto Nether Lane and follow its course to Goodbent Lodge.

Goodbent was a hunting lodge which was built and owned by a very wealthy Victorian family, called Senior who lived at Cliffe House in the village of Shepley, which lies approximately 5 miles to the east of Holmfirth.

Continuing along the lane for approximately 350 metres, you will arrive, once again, at the junction with Springs Road. From here, retrace your original steps along the Kirklees Way back to Wessenden Head.

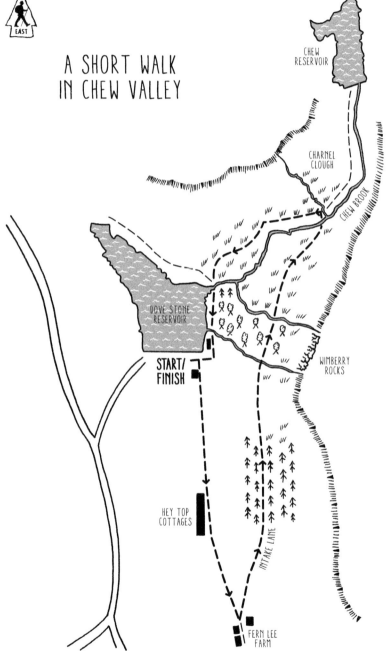

A SHORT WALK
IN CHEW VALLEY

EAST

CHEW
RESERVOIR

CHARNEL
CLOUGH

CHEW BROOK

DOVE STONE
RESERVOIR

START/
FINISH

WIMBERRY
ROCKS

HEY TOP
COTTAGES

INTAKE LANE

FERN LEE
FARM

A short walk in Chew Valley

Start/Finish: *Dove Stone car park, Bank Lane, Greenfield*
Grid Reference: *SD 013 034*
Distance: *5.7km/3.5 miles*
Ascent: *100 metres/328 feet*
Time: *2 hours*
OS Map: *Explorer OL1: The Dark Peak*

Introduction

This lovely short walk takes an easy to follow route around the beautiful and rugged Chew Valley. Suitable for walkers of all abilities, the route offers stunning views throughout and is an ideal option in foul weather or when time is limited.

Route in brief

Dove Stone Reservoir – Fern Lee Farm – Intake Lane – Chew Piece Plantation – Charnel Clough – Dove Stone Reservoir

Route Description

From the public toilets, proceed in a westerly direction along Bradbury Lane past several terraced cottages at Hey Top. Known as 'Forty Row', the cottages, which initially numbered 40 cramped back-to-back dwellings, were built for employees

at the nearby Greenfield Mill. Soon the lane peters out and becomes but a narrow track until it joins Intake Lane at Fern Lee Farm. Turning sharp left, follow the stony lane as it makes its way through a coniferous wood. If you pass through these woods at dawn or dusk you may be lucky enough to see a shy deer, emerging from deep within the silent forest.

After passing through the woods, cross the open field above Kinder Intake. To the south, below Wimberry Stones Brow, is the crash site of a British European Airways Douglas Dakota DC3.G-HACY which, on 19th August 1949, flew into the hillside, killing 24 passengers and crew. There are hundreds of similar crash sites across this area and throughout the Dark Peak, most of which occurred during the Second World War.

The route now continues through Chew Piece Plantation before crossing Rams Clough. This delightful beech wood is a fantastic spot in summer for family picnics, where children can let their imaginations unfold as they play amongst the trees and rocks. Lying along the plantation's eastern fringes are several large boulders that provide a popular playground for climbers.

With the sound of Chew Brook flowing along the valley bottom, make your way along the old tramway to the wooden bridge at the foot of Charnel Clough. In the early 1900s, a small railway line ran along here from Mossley, which transported stone and clay for the construction of Chew Reservoir, which sits at the head of the valley.

Upon reaching the reservoir access road, head downhill as a spectacular vista unfolds. Looking across Dove Stone Reservoir, Alderman Hill towers high above the valley, guarding the Holmfirth Road as it climbs steeply onto Saddleworth Moor.

At the bottom of the descent, bear left and, once again, cross Chew Brook on your return to the car park, which marks the end of a lovely short walk in the Chew Valley.

JOURNEYMAN

If you enjoyed reading this book and would like to be kept informed of future publications, please sign up for periodic updates and newsletters at:

www.saddleworthdiscoverywalks.co.uk

For the latest information follow us on facebook and twitter.

facebook.com/saddleworth.discoverywalks

twitter.com/walksaddleworth

Useful Information

The following is a list of shops, cafés, pubs and websites which may be useful.

Tourist Information

www.visitoldham.com

www.saddleworth.org.uk

Saddleworth Museum

www.saddleworthmuseum.co.uk

Saddleworth Historical Society

saddleworth-historical-society.org.uk

Pennine Waterways

www.penninewaterways.co.uk

Huddersfield Canal Society

www.huddersfieldcanal.com

Saddleworth Canal Cruises

www.saddleworth-canal-cruises.co.uk

Standedge Tunnel and Visitor Centre

canalrivertrust.org.uk/standedge-tunnel

Peak District National Park

peakdistrict.gov.uk

RSPB Dove Stone

rspb.org.uk/reserves/guide/d/dovestone/

National Trust

nationaltrust.org.uk/marsden-moor

Saddleworth Weather Forecast

bbc.co.uk/weather/2638879

Cafés

Also see individual routes for recommendations

Diggle

Diggle Chippy, 152 Huddersfield Road

Grandpa Greene's, 5 Ward Lane

www.grandpagreenes.co.uk

Delph

Delph Fish & Chip Shop,
25 King Street,

Saddleworth Arts co-operative
12 King Street,

Dobcross

The Garden Café, Newbank Garden Centre, Dobcross New Road

The Lime Kiln Café, Wool Road

www.thelimekilncafe.com

Uppermill

Christy's Coffee House,
38 High Street,

Java Bar Espresso,
73 High Street,

Kitty's Riverside Café Bar,
High Street,

Pubs

Also see individual routes for recommendations

Delph

The Kings Arms, Delph Road, Grains Bar

The Old Bell Inn, Huddersfield Road
www.theoldbellinn.co.uk

Royal Oak, Broad Lane, Heights

The Swan, King Street

The White Lion, Delph Lane

Denshaw

The Junction Inn, Rochdale Road
www.junctioninndenshaw.co.uk

The Rams Head, Ripponden Road
www.ramsheaddenshaw.co.uk

Dobcross

The Navigation, Wool Road

The Swan Inn, The Square
www.theswandobcross.com

Greenfield

The Clarence, Chew Valley Road

The King William IV, Chew Valley Road

The Royal George, Manchester Road

The Wellington, Chew Valley Road

Marsden

The Carriage House, Manchester Road, Standedge,
www.thecarriage-house.co.uk

The Great Western, Manchester Road, Standedge,

Uppermill

The Church Inn, Church Lane
www.churchinnsaddleworth.co.uk

The Commercial, High Street

The Cross Keys Inn, Running Hill Gate
www.crosskeysinn.co.uk

The Granby Arms, High Street

Hare and Hounds , High Street

The Waggon Inn, High Street

Outdoor Shops

Mountainfeet, Marsden, HD7 6AE
Grid: SE 051 117
www.mountainfeet.co.uk

Christian Maylor - *Author*

Christian Maylor was born and raised on a farm in Saddleworth
and has always had a passion for the outdoors. An experienced walker, fell runner
and cyclist, Chris has been lucky enough to travel throughout the world,
both for work and pleasure. His love for the hills, valleys and moors in and around
Saddleworth, which he developed as a young boy, has never waned,
and he is always drawn back to his home area.

This is Chris's first venture into guidebook writing, which he has fully enjoyed,
and he has plans to write others in the future.

www.saddleworthdiscoverywalks.co.uk

Ray Green - *Photographer*

Ray Green is a locally acclaimed photographer who lives in Saddleworth.
Having a passion for the outdoors, Ray specialises in landscape photography.
A keen fell runner and mountain biker, Ray enjoys capturing the
dramatically beautiful Saddleworth landscape.

www.raygreenphotography.co.uk

Acknowledgements

I would like to express my sincere gratitude to all those who have
helped with this project, in particular my family and friends, who have provided
essential encouragement and support.
Special thanks go to my wonderful son, Lewis, who accompanied me
on some of the walks; Ray Green for the amazing photographs;
Tony Greene Esq and my Dad for proofreading the initial drafts and for their
supportive feedback;
Rob Taylor for his invaluable advice about book design and layout;
Lee Copplestone for the original cover design;
Alastair Humphreys for his advice about publishing and pointing me
in the right direction;
and Tom Allen for his string of helpful emails.
Thanks also to my friends at Saddleworth Runners Club
for their fantastic company over the years, both on and off the hill.
Apologies if there is anyone I have forgotten to name.
You are no less thought of.

MAHDI.O.IDHAM

A percentage from the sale of this book
will be donated to Oldham Mountain Rescue Team and
Mahdlo Youth Zone (Oldham)

Dedicated to

Walter Maylor
My hero, my best friend, my grandad.
His stories awakened my thirst
for adventure.

Saddleworth
Discovery Walks
with **CHRISTIAN MAYLOR**

JOURNEYMAN

www.saddleworthdiscoverywalks.co.uk